# LEADING LAWYERS

A practical toolkit to help you adjust your leadership style and deliver great results

**SALLY SANDERSON**

First published in Great Britain by Practical Inspiration Publishing, 2021



ISBN 9781788602921 (print)
9781788602914 (epub)
9781788602907 (mobi)

To David, Tom and Nick

The beauty of the ABCDE model and toolkit is that it is simple but not simplistic, it's user-friendly and works in practice.

*Joanne Gubbay, Former Head of Learning and Development, Slaughter and May*

More than ever before, law firms need good leaders. However, leadership skills don't always get the attention they deserve, especially in early years of practice. I'm delighted to see how Sally has provided a simple and effective template to get every lawyer, junior or senior, thinking about the development that would make them a better leader of people. Having seen Sally run many development courses in the past, it is no surprise that the approach outlined in this book is very practical but also draws on theory and many years of observed behaviour in professional services, to make it a valuable tool in real life.

*Ben Tidswell, Chairman, Ashurst LLP*

I loved this book. It is so helpful to find a leadership book focused on the behaviour, personalities and scenarios found in law firms and with lawyers. The book is both thought provoking and highly practical with many realistic, tried and tested suggestions. It is useful for anyone who wishes to get the best out of others as a leader, coach, mentor or HR/Talent professional working with lawyers. This book is on our recommended reading list for all of our leaders.

*Yvonne Garricks, Head of Talent Development, Dentons UK, Ireland and Middle East LLP*

Good lawyers must make good leaders; or, so the old lie goes. Leadership, just like law, requires a framework that you can apply to situations, circumstances and individuals. *Leading Lawyers* is unique in that it provides both a complete toolkit and framework you can apply to your leadership, team and clients' position; and also a reference that you can dip into quickly for specific and effective advice and help on how to deal with a particular situation, client or team member based on how you and they work together. Lawyers should have this on their desk next to their favourite text book / internet legal search link.

*William James, Partner, Addleshaw Goddard LLP*

Amongst many books on leadership, this is a highly practical guide on how to work effectively with the different personalities. Sally elegantly extracts and combines the essence of various behavioural psychometric tools and gives you a simple 5-step process for leading others, managing up and down, giving feedback and managing projects. Without enormous effort, this can become part of your daily routine, and will help you form better relationships and deliver with the least friction.

*Neil May, Chief Operations Officer, Thackray Williams LLP*

Sally generously shares in her book a range of practical tools to support lawyers in their efforts to become effective leaders. Her unique insight into the leadership challenges faced by those in the legal world are derived from years of experience supporting and coaching legal practitioners in all stages of their career. Any lawyer who aspires to become a truly effective and inspiring leader should keep a copy of Sally's toolkit on their desk as a key resource when facing daily leadership challenges.

*Veronique Faucher, General Counsel and Global Head of Legal, REDEVCO*

I really enjoyed this book. It was obvious to me that Sally has worked with lawyers and understands the pressures and conflicting priorities that we face. The book provides sound practical advice for team and task management. Identifying your own style and that of the members of your team is an enlightening and extremely useful process allowing you to get the best out of yourself and others. I now use the ABCDE approach to plan my meetings.

*Simon Knott, Partner, Penningtons Manches Cooper LLP*

I have already followed the ABCDE toolkit this morning during my discussion with my Partner and it worked!

*Senior Associate, Magic Circle Firm*

Self-awareness is essential for effective leaders and 'Leading Lawyers' provides excellent guidance on achieving that state.

*Tony King, Lexington Consultants*

It is a painful truth for lawyers to discover, later on in their careers, that learning to lead other lawyers is every bit as demanding as learning the Law. This book saves time for busy lawyers by crystallising the key points in a framework that's easy to use and re-use and helping to rehearse the tricky conversations that all good leaders need to hold.

*Roger Wyn-Jones, Associate Fellow, Said Business School, Oxford University*

Much has been written about leadership in law firms, but few have been able to nail it down to the essentials and describe it in practical and pragmatic terms. Sally Sanderson of Profex Consulting has been coaching and training lawyers for more than 20 years throughout Europe. I had the pleasure of working with her while at Clifford Chance. In her new book and based on several – very recognizable – case studies she provides a practical toolkit for leading lawyers. Her **ABCDE**-model is **achievable, beneficial**, and very **clear**. A compelling and great book with practical insights, tips, and tools. An excellent guide for law firm leaders and those in leadership positions!

*Gerard Tanja, Partner, Venturis Consulting Group*

Sally adeptly links her experience in the legal profession with her knowledge of multiple psychometric tools, articulating how leadership development in this field can be enhanced through the self-awareness that psychometrics provide. I enjoyed how practical and accessible the recommendations were, helping to show how easy it can be to link theory to practice in the real world.

*Jayson Darby, Head of Science, Thomas International*

# Contents

# Introduction

## Why I wrote this book

I have worked with thousands of lawyers over the past 25 years and am always impressed by their drive to deliver for clients, their expertise, objectivity and intellect. However, I find that many struggle to have good quality conversations with their teams and team members. Why? It is partly because time is such a premium and the culture is clients first. However, it is also because lawyers are trained to be objective and to distrust some of the 'fuzzy' stuff that would help them lead, inspire, manage different personalities and deal with difficult conversations. In their daily life lawyers react, analyse, solve, advise and move on to the next matter. This objectivity and pace is at the expense of what helps us to lead. The more our brain builds our ability to analyse and synthesize facts, the less we use the neurones that enable us to empathize, to read others and adjust our conversation. Eventually, after years, those neural pathways get harder and harder to use or even die away.

By the time a lawyer starts to lead in a law firm, typically as a senior associate or partner, that process has taken its toll. They are an expert in their field but find that leadership is tricky and time-consuming, that 'people issues' are messy and that logic doesn't always win the day. Leadership, for many, proves far less satisfying than working with clients and so quickly slips down the to-do list and so conversations get squeezed or avoided.

This doesn't need to happen or be that difficult. With a little insight into your own personality and way of communicating, and a simple, logical model to help plan leadership conversations, you can be far more effective. I wrote this book to help lawyers understand their own leadership style and then use my simple model to plan better conversations. It is based on what I have learned coaching and developing lawyers, using psychometric profiling tools, and through trial and error. I want more lawyers to benefit from my experience in helping leaders be the best version of themselves.

In my coaching work I started to notice that leaders in law firms often miss out key bits of a leadership conversation and that this was linked to their personality. They prioritized some things they need to say to direct, inspire and keep things on track, but missed out others. It was over several years of listening to and coaching partners that I developed the **ABCDE** model in this book. Leaders I have coached have used it to have better conversations with their teams about their deals and cases and with individuals about their performance.

Why one model? On leadership development programmes, I found many lawyers like theoretical models (as do I) but they soon forget them and then can't apply them in practice. So, it's a waste. The aim of this book is to give you one model that is simple and memorable and which can be used for a wide range of team conversations. It should save you time as well as make you a more effective leader. As you get more familiar with it, you can do it in the moment.

It is also a model you can personalize – by spotting which bits of leadership conversations you are likely to omit because of your personality preferences, you can easily learn to include the missing letter/s – whether **A**, **B**, **C**, **D** or **E**.

Likewise, you can personalize it for team members. If you recognize their personality preferences and the bits of **ABCDE** that are important for them – and sections they too might neglect – it is easier to inspire them, align them and communicate on their wavelength. In this way you can adjust to different personalities and enable them to deliver better results.

## Who this book is for

As a leader in a law firm your reputation depends not so much on what you do, but on what you enable your team to deliver. The aim of this book is to enhance your communications so your team achieves fantastic results.

If you are known as a leader who directs, inspires and supports teams you will find it easier to tap into talent and compete for resource – whether that's people or budget. Associates and paralegals want to work on successful teams and to work with great team leaders. They can be adept at avoiding those who have a reputation of being a nightmare leader!

This book is for you if you are a lawyer and:

- You want to find out how your own personality affects the way you lead a team. You want to adjust your leadership style – you know you are too pushy or too nice or too controlling and want some tips on how to get a better balance.
- You lead a team which needs to deliver for demanding clients – whether internal or external. Expectations are high yet your team is lean: you need everyone to give that little bit more.
- You want to improve your team's motivation; you want to bring out the best in individuals and you want to tackle performance problems in a direct but supportive way.
- You find it difficult to get through to some members of your team – they don't get you and what you are trying to do – and you just don't understand them.
- You manage big transactions or cases and have mastered the project management process but find that too often 'people issues' get in the way. You need to find a way of getting team members to follow the plan so you can deliver on time and on budget.
- You'd like to assess your personal leadership style or you have already completed a DISC, Insights Discovery®[1] or Social Styles behavioural style profile and you want some practical tools to help you be more effective as a team leader.
- You want one simple model to help you plan motivating conversations – that ensures you cover all the ground not just what you would instinctively focus on.
- You want some tools to help you plan specific conversations with your team.

## Why read this book

This book aims to make you a more effective leader. It will help you adjust your style so you play to your strengths and avoid traps which unaware leaders fall into.

[1] Insights Discovery® is a registered trade mark of The Insights Group Limited.

It will save you time, help you deliver better results and enhance your reputation.

You will learn the five things you need to communicate to your team – the **ABCDE** way of leading. Although this may seem simple, you will discover why different personalities focus on some elements of the message at the expense of others. You will identify your own communication preferences and how these affect the **ABCDE** of your leadership style – both your strengths and the things you need to work on.

You will also discover ways of getting different personalities on board – in your team, your boss and clients – by understanding what they are looking for from you and what they want to hear when you are communicating with them.

To make this practical, you will find a series of tools using the **ABCDE** model for planning project conversations and to help you discuss performance with individuals in your team.

Each step of the way there are examples to inspire you and opportunities to plan how to use the approach in practice, so you become an even more effective team leader.

## How to use this book

This book is set out in six parts:

### Part 1: Leading is as easy as ABCDE

Provides an overview of the **ABCDE** model which helps leaders to get better results from their teams. Then each section of the model is explored in detail with opportunities for you to do some planning on how to use it in practice. If you have never considered your own personality preferences, after the Introduction to Part 1 you might like to turn to Part 2 before reading the detail in Chapters 1–5.

### Part 2: Your leadership style

This part explores different leadership styles and how they link to the **ABCDE** model. It should help you to identify your own style preferences and how to fine-tune your approach. We start by looking at leaders with a very clear style where one personality preference dominates their way of communicating. But most people have more than one preference in their style, so we look at a range of leaders commonly found in law firms who represent a combination of two or three preferences. You may well recognize the style of some of the case study leaders.

## Part 3: Aligning different personalities

This part gives you some tips on how to work with and align those with different personalities – whether a team member, a boss or a client. It will help you to adapt your own style when you need to motivate, influence and manage others who don't share the same style as you. It will make you aware of which parts of the **ABCDE** message different personalities listen out for, which parts motivate them and which parts they might ignore, which could lead to lower levels of performance or support. After the introduction you can turn to the chapters covering the types of personality you find most challenging to lead.

## Part 4: Tools for project conversations

This is the first of two **ABCDE** toolkits for you to use when needed. It provides a series of **ABCDE** conversation tools to help you in different situations where you are leading and managing a project team – whether for clients or for internal projects such as for business development. Tools include scoping and planning, briefing the team, delegating part of a project, reviewing progress, reporting to stakeholders and conducting an end of project/matter review.

## Part 5: Tools for one-to-one performance conversations

The second **ABCDE** toolkit focuses on the conversations that leaders have with individual team members from when they join the team through to delegating, praising, coaching, tackling problems, performance reviews and development planning. Whether a team member is a high flyer, a solid performer or struggling, you can adapt these tools to give them the support they need to deliver their best. Again, refer to these tools when you need them.

## Part 6: Conclusion and next steps

By the end of the book you should have identified some adjustments to make to your leadership style and some go-to tools to help you get better results. You now need to turn your good intentions into leadership habits. Therefore, we close with some practical self-coaching tips and other ideas to help you embed your changes.

## Appendix 1: Completing a behavioural profile

This appendix gives you some links to personal profiling assessments which are compatible with the **ABCDE** model: DISC (Personal Profile Analysis), Insights Discovery® and Social Styles.

## Appendix 2: ABCDE Planner

This is a collection of the planning exercises introduced in Part 1 so that you can use them whenever you are planning a project or an initiative.

## Appendix 3: Additional resources

This includes some suggestions for further reading and additional resources.

## About the case studies

The case studies in the book are based on my experience of working with leaders in law firms and in-house legal teams. Each, however, is an amalgamation of more than one situation, more than one person and facts have been adapted – so they are fictitious and no resemblance to real life partners or leaders is intended. They are often presented without gender (and I use 'they' as the pronoun instead of 'he/she') and from diverse backgrounds. The aim is to illustrate what happens in practice across the legal globe and to help readers identify with common challenges that lawyers face.

# Part 1

# Leading is as easy as ABCDE

# Introduction

## What leaders need to do to deliver great results

When coaching team leaders in law firms, I noticed that different personalities would have different issues when leading their teams:

- Some were stuck in the detail and were not clear on what they wanted to achieve
- Some were very negative and struggled to enthuse others
- Some were too hands-off and did not consider the steps to complete the work
- Some were too optimistic and did not plan how to manage risks
- And most were so busy that they did not stop and review what they had done or learn lessons for next time.

Listening to them talk I noticed that they had a communication pattern of emphasizing or focusing on only a couple of the things that team leaders need to do – rarely did they cover everything. This left gaps for their teams to fill in. Some teams are great at filling in those gaps, but others may not know how, may not be willing or, in extreme cases, not allowed to do so.

> One senior associate was so frustrated by their partner failing to set direction that when I met them, they were trying to get off the team to work on another case. The partner was leading a very complex investigation with input from several teams in different jurisdictions. In their office they had a large whiteboard on which they had mapped out all the information flows, the steps that needed to be taken and by when. They held regular update calls with the team. All good, but it was frustratingly slow and unclear where they were headed. They weren't taking time out from 'doing the work' to plan the strategy for the case. They

were not a big picture thinker and they were lost in the detail and the process. The senior associate could see what was missing and the impact it was having on the investigation. We developed a simple solution: they held a weekly strategy meeting with the partner before the weekly team update – that way the partner got into the habit of stepping back from the detail and focusing on end results. Team calls became more focused, the investigation moved faster and the senior associate started to enjoy the project. If the partner had been more aware of their personal strengths and weaknesses as a leader this could have been avoided. They needed the **ABCDE** tool.

It was over several years of listening to and coaching team leaders that I developed the **ABCDE** tool to help lawyers cover all the things they need to do when leading teams:

1. Set direction for the team
2. Get and keep the team enthused
3. Ensure the team knows what steps to take and when
4. Help the team avoid problems and manage risks
5. Monitor progress and outcomes.

Here it is and why different personalities tend to prioritize different elements of the model:

| | |
|---|---|
| A | Achieve - the end results we need to deliver |
| B | Benefits - why and for whom this is important |
| C | Clarify how - the steps we need to take |
| D | Difficulties - how we will avoid these |
| E | Evaluate - our progress and outcomes |

**Achieve:** First we must talk to our teams about what we need to achieve. Highly directive leaders will naturally emphasize this. Goal oriented team members are listening out for this. What's the challenge? What do we need to do to win? What do we need to prioritize? This is where big picture thinkers start (and sometimes finish!)

**Benefits:** Next we need to get our team enthused about what we want them to do. Inspiring team leaders know that to get their teams to work harder, they sell the idea to them. Leadership is a trade – if you work hard for me, this is what I'll give you in return. For some team members this is critical – they want to be inspired, enthused, excited; they want to feel that they chose to get involved, that this project is important for them and their career.

**Clarify how**: Then we need to be clear about what is going to happen, the steps we need the team to take to achieve the goal. Practical team leaders will focus on the steps, the process to be followed. They will give their team a project plan or a checklist to follow. Some team members will distrust a big idea until the leader can demonstrate that they have thought it through and planned what needs to happen. They will be more reluctant to start until they know what is required.

**Difficulties to avoid:** Not everything goes as smoothly as planned so we also need to anticipate what could go wrong and take action to prevent it. Cautious team leaders will have this at the front of their mind, but optimists often neglect this. Cautious personalities are risk managers and problem solvers; they will emphasize the difficulties that need to be overcome. For cautious team members this will be reassuring – they also will be thinking of what could go wrong and they resent being set up for failure by a leader who hasn't anticipated the rocks ahead.

**Evaluate progress and outcomes:** Finally, once the team gets working, all leaders need to ensure that the team is making steady progress. Some leaders are initiators but not good at follow-up and we all know that what gets measured, gets done. It is critical that all leaders tell their team how they are going to monitor and evaluate progress so that the team knows that the project or the idea won't fizzle out and that they will get the leader's support during implementation.

## Where's your focus?

When you are talking what do you prioritize? Where do you start and where do you finish? Do you start in a rush of excitement or do you start with how difficult this project is going to be? What we start with and focus on is likely to reflect our personal style – but it might not reflect what our teams want to hear from us. Planning how to supplement our preferred communication style helps us to be more effective and to work around our personal limitations. It is rare for a team leader to instinctively cover all the five elements in the **ABCDE** tool simply because different personality preferences make these steps mutually exclusive. If you are naturally cautious, it is likely you'll feel less comfortable trying to inspire others. If you are a big picture thinker, it is likely you will be impatient with detail. These personal preferences and how they affect leadership style are explained in Part 2.

Effective leaders are self-aware of their strengths and the corresponding weaknesses. With awareness they can plan to change their behaviours or work around their limitations. Some leaders know that to be effective they need a co-leader.

> I worked with a practice group leader who was visionary but a terrible communicator. He was strategic and could spot an opportunity in the market and how to position the practice to take advantage of it. However, he was no good at selling the idea to the other more cautious partners in the team. He didn't see the need to persuade them when to him it was so logical and obvious what needed to be done. Over several years he had come to rely on a co-leader – the youngest partner and the only woman in the team. She knew how to communicate his plans to others. She was enthusiastic, practical and patient. She spent time listening to the partners' concerns and explaining the practical steps that would need to be taken. Without her, his strategy would not have got off the ground and it wouldn't be the successful practice it is today. They made a formidable pair.

However, you may not have the ideal co-leader to cover the bits you don't like doing. This book will show you how to use the **ABCDE** model in a range of situations so that your team and the individuals in your team excel.

Are you already aware of your own style? Many lawyers have completed a personality or behavioural profile. There are many different diagnostic tools on the market. I have focused on DISC, Insights Discovery® and Social Styles behavioural profiles as millions have taken these, they are widely used in law firms and their four quadrant models are easy to understand. If you have taken one of these, the following table is for quick reference as to how these link with the **ABCDE** model. Then as you read through the detailed sections on **ABCDE** you can link it to your own preferences. You may well have one or more preferences in your style – look for what is missing in your profile.

Different steps in the **ABCDE** are prioritized by those with the following preferences:

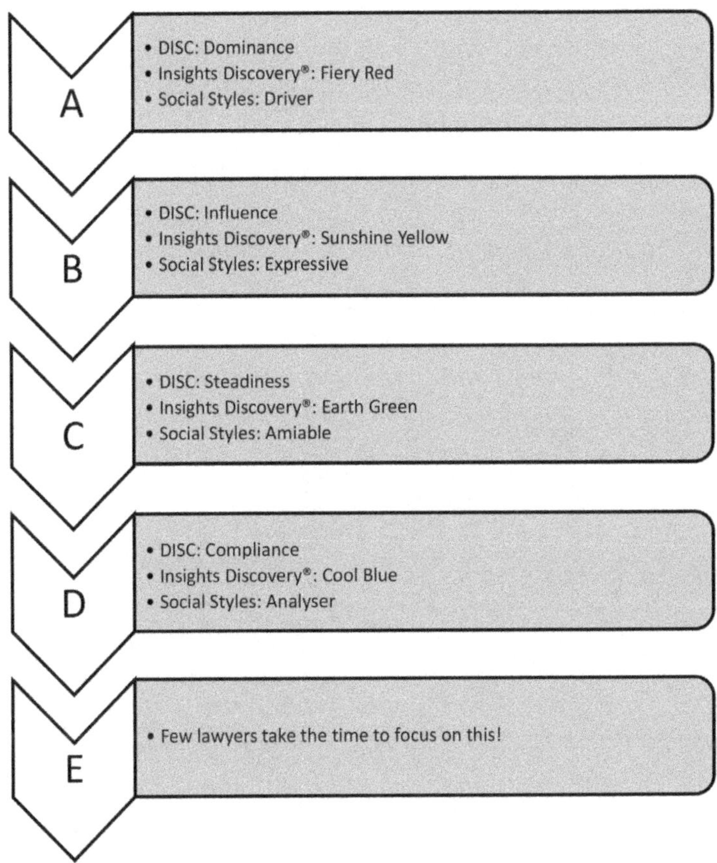

Some law firms favour other profiling tools such as MBTI (Myers-Briggs Typology Inventory), 16PF or Hogan Development Survey. These are all good and valid (I use them in my coaching too) but are not quite so easy to map directly against the **ABCDE** model. If you have had feedback based on another profiling tool, you can still use the insights you gained to link your likely behaviours to the leadership behaviours discussed in this book in Part 2.

If you have never completed a profile and would like to work out your own focus before reading more about each section of the **ABCDE** model, you can either:

1. Turn to Part 2 to identify your style or
2. Turn to Appendix 1 for how to complete a behavioural profile.

# Chapter 1

# Achieve

## Why

We all need to know where we are going. We look to a leader to focus our efforts on what we need to achieve. Without this direction we would all work inefficiently aiming at different things. Alternatively, we might lack the drive to deliver exceptional results.

Having a clear target or goal is critical to our motivation. As a team leader you need to set clear goals for fee earning work and to translate business strategy into project or task goals that make sense for your team on a day-to-day basis. This gives us purpose and certainty as to what we need to do in order to do a good job.[2]

When we set direction for our teams, we make our expectations clear. This is the push, the demanding part of leadership. As a team leader you are telling your team:

- This is what I'm expecting of you
- This is what I want you to achieve
- This is what good performance looks like
- This is what success will look like.

It is a challenge to the team to deliver great results. It is also easier to have a difficult conversation with a team member who isn't performing

---

[2] Goal setting has been widely researched in industrial and organizational psychology and The Centre for Evidence-Based Management's research found that 'setting challenging, specific goals leads to higher performance than urging people to do their best and this positive effect is present in both self-set and assigned goals as well as individual and group goals.' (*Rapid evidence assessment of the research literature on the effect of goal setting on workplace performance, CIPD Technical Report, December 2016, page 13*).

or a team which isn't delivering if we have mapped out our expectations clearly upfront.

Some people are naturally very goal focused and demanding of themselves and others. They are driven by goals and targets and expect their teams to be too. However, many of us are less goal oriented – for example, we may not have written down career goals – and we tend to focus more on the process, or working effectively with others or pleasing clients, rather than the outcome.[3] If you are a leader without a strong achievement orientation, it is very easy to neglect talking to your team about the end goal, the results they need to achieve.

Have you ever felt the frustration of being unclear about what is expected of you – what the end game is? I come across this frequently when I am coaching people.

A brilliant lawyer coming up for partnership was referred to me for coaching because they weren't making sufficient progress with business development. Probing the causes, it became apparent that they were hesitant to invest lots of time and effort since they were unclear as to the future direction of the practice. They were literally stalled. They had seen the partners huddled behind closed doors planning their group strategy – but they hadn't shared their thinking with the lawyer or any of the team at all. You can imagine how this left the team feeling – unsure and insecure.

Some leaders will say they can't provide much clarity – they need to see how things work out, what markets, clients or top management will do. However, as leaders we need to set at least a general sense of direction for the team. We can tell them we are 'heading North' even if we haven't yet decided which city will be

[3] David McClelland's motivation theory suggests that Achievement (a strong drive to accomplish goals) is one of three main motivators for people. The other two are Affiliation (wanting to work in a group and be liked) and Power (wanting to have power and influence over others). Each of us will have one of these as a dominant motivator and this is largely dependent on our culture and life experiences. McClelland, D., *The Achieving Society* (D. Van Nostrand Company 1961, reprint available from Pickle Partners Publishing).

our ultimate destination. If we have a sense of the general direction it means we exclude other distracting options. We can narrow our focus and pull together as a team.

We now know from neuroscience that providing a sense of direction and purpose isn't just good leadership – it activates our caveman brain into action, specifically the amygdala and limbic system which is linked to our primal survival mechanisms.[4] Situations where there is a lack of certainty or clarity about what is going to happen make us anxious. Our primal brain perceives them as a threat, as if it is a matter of basic survival: Will I stay safe? Where is my next meal going to come from? Once we feel threatened, we will behave to protect ourselves. At work this might result in behaviours such as keeping quiet in meetings, avoiding taking responsibility, prioritizing lower-level tasks where success is guaranteed or focusing efforts where the outcome is more certain.[5]

A leader who provides a strong sense of direction, is clear on goals and purpose, provides a reward trigger for the caveman brain – something to go towards. The team member is more certain about what needs to be achieved and is motivated to work towards that goal and so will contribute more.

## How

When coaching lawyers, I have found that many struggle to articulate a clear ***Achieve*** statement whether for briefing a team, delegating or

---

[4] David Rock in *Your Brain at Work* has listed the triggers for our caveman brain at work in a useful and memorable model for leaders: SCARF which stands for Status, Certainty, Autonomy, Relatedness, and Fairness. As leaders, when we are interacting with our teams we need to remember to use these five triggers as motivators, by providing opportunities to enhance Status, providing Certainty, increasing Autonomy where we can, Relating to our teams and acting Fairly. Failure to do this can make our teams feel threatened and they will behave defensively. Rock, D., *Your Brain at Work* (Harper Collins, 2009).

[5] 'Uncertainty registers (in a part of the brain called the anterior cingulate cortex) as an error, gap or tension: something that must be corrected before we can feel comfortable again. That is why people crave certainty. Not knowing what will happen next can be profoundly debilitating because it requires extra neural energy. This diminishes energy, undermines performance, and disengages people from the present.' Rock, D., 'Managing with the Brain in Mind', *strategy+business Issue 56,* Autumn 2009, Reprint 09206.

giving feedback. Effective ***Achieve*** statements take time to craft and they are most effective when:

- Short – expressed in fewer than 20 words
- Positively expressed
- Specific
- Tangible
- Include an indicator or measure of success.

To create your ***Achieve*** statement ask yourself the following questions:

- What's the end goal?
- What tangible result does the team or team member need to achieve?
- What will be an indicator that the team or person has succeeded?

Example ***Achieve*** statements:

- We need to complete this transaction for £500K by 3 June.
- We need to double our market share of this client's work.
- We need to introduce this project management software by year end.
- We need to increase the profit margin of our fixed fee work by 10%.
- We need to win two new media tech clients by the end of the financial year.
- We need to run six client seminars to raise our profile in the oil and gas sector.
- We need to increase our pitch conversion rate to 60%.
- We need to plan how to apply our expertise to the pharmaceutical sector by year end.
- I want to help you double the amount you delegate to associates on the next project.
- I'd like to see you become the go-to contact for client x by the end of the year.

## Apply: *Achieve* planner

Apply this to your own situation. At the end of each chapter in Part 1 you will have the opportunity to apply the thinking to a real life project. Choose something that is important to you and where you need to get a team on board. It might be a project you have already started. It might be a client project, a business development project or an improvement you want to introduce.

One of the early reviewers of this book had been trying to implement a new marketing strategy with his team but it wasn't going as well as he had anticipated. He said he found these application exercises extremely helpful in processing the **ABCDE** information and, by applying it to his project, he gained practical insights that helped him overcome the blocks he was facing.

Thinking of your project or the improvement you want to make, describe what you want it to ***Achieve*** in fewer than 20 words. (At this stage don't include why this goal is important.)

Now review your ***Achieve*** statement – is it:

- ✓ Succinct?
- ✓ Clear about the end result or goal?
- ✓ Specific?
- ✓ Tangible?
- ✓ Challenging but realistic?
- ✓ Positively expressed?
- ✓ Does it include an indicator of success?
- ✓ Will it be possible to monitor progress towards it?

# Chapter 2

# Benefits

## Why

Once you've told your team where they are headed and what you want them to ***Achieve***, you need to enthuse them for the journey by explaining the ***Benefits***. Together they will give a strong sense of purpose.[6]

You need to explain why the task is important – how it will help the client, the team, your firm and the individuals in the team too. Show how it links to your values – whether that's for service excellence, innovative thinking, trusted relationships, etc.

Your team members will all have some degree of choice as to how much effort they apply to any project. They could do just enough to avoid trouble or they could choose to go all out to make the project successful. Your job is to inspire them to put in this discretionary effort.

Often you will be competing for their attention. They may work on multiple matters or projects for several people. Why should they want to prioritize your project and put their best efforts at your disposal?

Spending time explaining the importance of the project to the client and different stakeholders will give them a sense of purpose beyond themselves and an understanding of where their contribution is going to make a difference. Usually this means you need to give the context and background to the project including the client's commercial objectives.

---

[6] Daniel Pink in *Drive: The Surprising Truth about What Motivates Us* identifies Purpose as a motivator which helps people achieve more, especially if linked to doing something important beyond themselves. Pink, D. H., *Drive: The Surprising Truth about What Motivates Us* (Riverhead Books, Penguin, 2009).

One inexperienced lawyer described how they had worked flat out for a week on a matter without having been told the name of the client or why this was an important piece of work. They were just given a task to get done by a challenging deadline. This wasn't because it was confidential but just because the supervisor hadn't thought it necessary and didn't have time to explain. With no understanding of the client or the client's commercial objectives it was difficult for the team member to get excited about what they were doing, and they resented the late nights. The team member couldn't see where their work was making a difference.

You also need to tell the team why the project is important for the team and your firm – this can seem obvious: pleasing the client to guarantee the next piece of work; ensuring the team meets its fee target; protecting the team's reputation internally or in the market; implementing a strategy. However, remember you are competing for their attention so why is this project as or more important to the team or your organization than others? Make the case, even if you only need to do so briefly.

Finally, where we can, we need to demonstrate the benefits to individual team members of working on the project. Put yourself in their shoes and think. What's in it for them? What will they get in return for their hard work? Drawing their salary isn't sufficient! It might be different things for different team members. It could be the opportunity to:

- Learn a new skill
- Develop new expertise
- Work for a client they admire
- Get experience in a new sector
- Take responsibility for a workstream
- Develop a track record
- Raise their profile internally or in the market
- Work with a new team
- Earn the right to work on a more interesting project/next stage of the project
- Work on something that is in-line with their personal values.

To do this effectively it helps if you know what interests and motivates your team members. In some of my workshops I ask team leaders to think of one team member and then write down the three things that the team member most wants to achieve over the next three to six months at work. Try it yourself.

1.

2.

3.

Can you list their work aspirations or are you having to guess? Usually about 50% of the team leaders I work with can't do this. Their pens hover. They are stuck because they haven't discussed this, ever. They just assume that the team member will want the same things as they want. But we are all different. Not knowing makes it impossible for the team leader to tap into their motivations – to align what their team member wants with the results the team leader needs to deliver.

One boss did this brilliantly with me. They made it easy to talk about what I wanted to achieve at work. I remember them saying, 'You ought to be aiming for my job in a couple of years. The problem is I don't intend to move on so let's talk about what you want to do. We can then plan the experience you need to get so you can land that role in another organisation.' You can imagine how having this honest conversation made it easy to ask me to go above and beyond – they put opportunities my way which helped me to develop a track record that would act as a stepping stone to my next career move.

Similarly, have you ever discussed your own and their values? How well do these link with your firm's values – if you have them? Although lawyers are often quite cynical about stated values, I usually find that an individual will have a strong sense of how they want to interpret their firm's values to link with their own personal values. When it is relevant to a project or task you want them to do, it can be highly motivating to mention their values and say that you know this is important to them.

If you show you have thought about benefits from the individual's perspective, you show that you care about them and are treating them like a human being rather than just a lump of resource to throw at a project. Leadership is more than a transaction – if you do this for me, this is what I will do for you. When we show we care about them, their contribution, job satisfaction, career opportunities and their values, we demonstrate empathy and relate to them on a human level. Our caveman brain responds positively, we feel like we belong and are safe, and so we feel more engaged.[7]

I worked with a practice group leader who was very motivated, ambitious and competitive but who was not good at relating to their team. They were impatient with them and could not understand the lack of drive shown by some of the very hard-working and able senior team members to go out and help build the practice. They rarely engaged with these team members on a one-to-one basis except to answer technical issues. Overall, the practice group leader had never shown them that they cared about their futures – growing the practice was all about being better than other teams in the firm and making the practice group leader look good. However, they could not grow the practice in the way they wanted on their own. They wanted four senior team members to each take responsibility for growing one workstream, but the practice group leader thought they would not rise to the

[7] In David Rock's SCARF model on primary threat and reward triggers for the brain, the R stands for Relatedness when we demonstrate empathy and relate to someone on a human level. Oxytocin is a brain chemical that is released when we experience close relations with others, and it generates a feeling of pleasure. It is present at birth and helps bind the close physical relationship with the mother, and it has also been identified in subjects when in collaborative conversation. Oxytocin release enhances aspects of the brain's functioning. Blood pressure lowers, the limbic relaxes and these create a state of enhanced cognitive flexibility – we are better able to see other perspectives. Rock, D., *Your Brain at Work* (Harper Collins, 2009).

challenge. We planned a meeting for them to spell out their vision to the four team members. They told them what they wanted to achieve and the roles they wanted them to play. For the first time they explicitly linked this to the benefits for them: an opportunity to fast track developing their own expertise in a workstream, so they would develop a name in the market, helping them to win work and create opportunities for partnership. They followed this with a one-to-one meeting with each of the team members to find out which workstream they wanted to lead, where they wanted to get involved and to help them start to put together a business development plan. Within a few years, the practice had grown and three of the four had made partner.

## How

To identify a ***Benefit***, use the 'so what' challenge. Describe why something is important and then challenge its relevance by saying 'So what? Why would they care?'. Find a WIIFM (What's In It For Me) by using the bridging phrase 'So what that means for you'. Here are three examples:

1. 'This is important for the client because they want to increase their market share.'

   ***So what?***

   'So what that means for us is they will have more deals in the pipeline for us to work on.'

   ***So what?***

   'Which is important as it means we will hit our target.'

   ***So what that means for you is?***

   'Our success will be recognized by the firm's board/we'll share in the bonus/we'll be able to recruit more help.'

2. 'We need to make this piece of work profitable.'

   ***So what?***

   'So we make a bigger contribution to the firm's profits.'

   ***So what that means for you is?***

   'It will help us retain our talented people/recruit an additional team member/have a bonus pot to share at the end of the year/ we can invest in upgrading our technology to make our job easier.'

3. 'This project will help you raise your profile with the client.'

   ***So what?***

   'So that means the client will start to come directly to you with questions and start to see you as a key adviser.'

   ***So what that means for you is?***

   'It will be the start of building a stronger relationship which will help you to win more work from that client and help you build the business case for partnership.'

To make a powerful case:

- Identify how different stakeholders will benefit from the work
- Paint a picture
- Link the importance to something the team member values
- Use the 'so what this means for you' bridging phrase
- Provide evidence that the benefits are real and can be delivered.

## Apply: *Benefits* planner

Still thinking of the project you used for the application exercise in Chapter 1, now list the benefits to different stakeholders – why it is so important.

| To the client/internal client: |
|---|
| |
| To the firm/your organization: |
| |
| To the team: |
| |
| To team members: |
| |

Now review your ***Benefits*** statements – do they:

- ✓ Overall, create a compelling sense of purpose for the team?
- ✓ Align to what is important to each stakeholder?
- ✓ Avoid any conflict of interest between different stakeholders?
- ✓ Describe something tangible or paint a picture such as:
  - Achievement of goals or values?
  - Return on investment?
  - Saved time?
  - Increased revenue or saved costs?
  - Decreased risk or hassle?
  - Improved market share, reputation or profile?
- ✓ Would it pass the test of a sceptic – can you provide proof?

# Chapter 3

# Clarify how

## Why

If you have been clear on the results you need to ***Achieve*** and have sold the ***Benefits*** to the team, they should be eager to start on the project. Assuming that you are not asking them to just continue with business as usual, then the next thing you need to do is ***Clarify how*** you want them to complete the work. This might mean you set out the steps you want the team to take or you might ask the team to work this out for themselves if they are experienced.

Team leaders who are familiar with project management will find the ***Clarify how*** part of the **ABCDE** model easy. They will be used to clarifying the steps to take by:

- Scoping the work (including what is excluded from the scope)
- Breaking down a project into manageable stages
- Creating timetables with interim deadlines and milestones
- Allocating roles and responsibilities
- Agreeing communication and decision-making protocols for co-ordinating and progressing the work
- Creating resource and budget plans.

However, in law firms many team leaders have not had the benefit of learning these skills and so they may underestimate the amount of planning that needs to be done on a project. For the team this can seem as if they are constantly battling against unrealistic expectations or dealing with chaos.

A leader was trying to build a practice of higher value work for their team. They complained that the team were not motivated and were not doing anything to help develop this new line of work – just continuing with existing work. The leader was rushing around doing lots of business development activities and believed setting an example was sufficient to demonstrate what they wanted. This left them no time for leading or managing the team. Talking to the leader it was very clear that although the team were aware of the overall aim to get higher value work, the leader had not agreed individual goals, had done nothing to motivate them and there were no plans. In fact, the leader had done no planning at all other than to identify the optimum size of instruction or type of assignment. Each month they held a quick meeting to report on the numbers and tell the team they weren't making sufficient progress. At these, the leader cut short any questions or debate about how they achieve this. They were a big picture thinker and not a natural planner. Before attending the leadership programme, the leader thought plans were low level administration; they did not recognize the team's need for a plan and did not even use agendas. It was easy to solve this by just investing a little more time in planning meetings where the leader could clarify what they wanted the team to do and help them develop their own ideas into action plans for winning higher value work.

At the other extreme, I also find some team leaders are over-prescriptive in clarifying how they want a project or task completed. Usually, they have been promoted because they are excellent at executing tasks themselves and so when leading a team, they seek to showcase this by providing detailed instructions as to how to do the work. This is well intentioned – they want to help their team. However, often the team experience this as micro-management and they can get frustrated, especially if they are experienced and want to demonstrate their capability to deliver. Moreover, such team leaders soon find that they run out of time to do the things they should be focusing on.

So why do some people over plan and others miss this out? A team leader's personality has a big impact here. An impatient, big picture thinker is likely to skip the project planning phase and leave the team swimming or sinking on their own. A perfectionist who finds it difficult to trust others is likely to be too controlling and will use so many directions that the team will be guided every step of the way, as if by satellite navigation (personal navigation system).

Therefore, we need to be aware of our own style preference and how it affects our approach to giving instructions and supervision. Before clarifying how the work should be done, a leader needs to stop and consciously select the right supervision approach to use. Choosing the right one will ensure the team can deliver, will motivate them, help them learn and take ownership. It will also save the leader time and ensure matters run more smoothly and are more profitable.

## How

The supervision approach you select is based on how much you trust your team/team member. For lawyers, this is mostly about whether the team/team member is sufficiently experienced. However, leaders often tell me of their frustration when an experienced team has failed to deliver. This is usually because the leader, relying on the team's experience, has left them to get on with it without checking progress or providing support when needed. As well as considering experience, you need to ask yourself:

- Can I trust them to prioritize this over other matters?
- Will they be confident to work on their own without my support?
- Will they be keen to learn and think for themselves?

Considering these questions will help you balance how much autonomy to give the team with how much certainty they need before proceeding.[8] This has a strong impact on motivation. Think about it

---

[8] Daniel Pink, in *Drive: The Surprising Truth about What Motivates Us*, identifies Autonomy as one of the three motivators for people today, especially in work contexts where teams need to be creative or solve complex problems. Pink, D. H., *Drive: The Surprising Truth about What Motivates Us* (Riverhead Books, Penguin, 2009). In David Rock's SCARF model of the brain's reward/threat triggers, Autonomy (the A) needs to be balanced with Certainty (the C). Rock, D., *Your Brain at Work* (Harper Collins, 2009).

from a team member's perspective. If I'm inexperienced and uncertain how to proceed, I'm not yet ready for autonomy and if given too much, I may become anxious that I will sink. Whereas, if I'm experienced and clear about what I need to achieve, then it is more motivating to be allowed to choose how I think it best to deliver.

Here are the five supervision approaches for lawyers which address the different factors affecting trust:

| **Inexperienced** | | **Experienced** | | |
|---|---|---|---|---|
| **Train/tell (sat nav)** | **Brainstorm and coach** | **Reassure** | **Motivate/sell** | **Delegate and let go** |
| Use for novices, when they don't know where or how to start. | Use for keen learners who have a little experience on which to build. | Use for cautious intermediates. You can trust them to know what to do, but they lack confidence to act independently. | Use for jaded experts or those juggling conflicting priorities. They know what to do but you can't trust them to get it done on time or to the standard required. | Use for self-reliant experts. You can trust them as they are experienced, confident and motivated to get it done. |
| Maximum supervision | | ⟷ | | Minimum supervision |
| Minimum autonomy | | | | Maximum autonomy |
| Hands-on | | | | Hands-off |

For those **who don't have sufficient experience to create their own plan**, there are two approaches you can take. You can tell them how to do it or you can get them thinking for themselves.

### 1. Train/tell (sat nav):

When you have a team or team member with no experience you are going to have to train them by giving them a detailed plan of how to proceed and then check they are following it every step of the way. The leader is acting like satellite navigation and this can be very comforting for both leader and team – everyone is clear what needs to be done and how to get there. However, it is very time-consuming for the leader and they need to be accessible 24/7 to the team to provide directions when needed or otherwise the project stalls.

Despite it being time-consuming, when a leader is time-poor it can be tempting to use this approach at the start of a project even when a team no longer needs it. The leader thinks it will get the team going quickly and approaching the project in precisely the way the leader would do it. However, this can make the team passive, just as we are when we follow satellite navigation directions. Over reliance on the sat nav to do the thinking for you means when we next do the same journey, we will still need the sat nav. In the same way a leader can inadvertently train a team or team member to rely on being given directions. In the short term it seems efficient but the next time they do a similar piece of work they will come back to the leader for instructions again. This becomes a drain on the leader's own time and energy. Lawyers are bright, that's why you hired them, so it is more interesting and motivating for them to have the opportunity to think for themselves.

Occasionally, in a real crisis, you might also need to adopt this approach. However, don't use this as an excuse for using sat nav all the time. Lawyers are always under time and cost pressure in the short term, but longer term you'll benefit if you have developed your team members so they require less input from you.

**2. Brainstorm and coach:**

To get **inexperienced** teams or team members thinking for themselves, start by brainstorming a plan together and use questions to help them think through the steps they need to take. This is a coaching approach where you are developing their thinking, rather than telling them what to think. Don't worry if they don't get it right or get stuck, that's when you step in and provide your input. They will appreciate the time you are investing and the expertise you share even more, because the process helps them recognize what they know and what they don't.

Turn what you would tell them into questions that start with 'what' and 'how' such as:

- What do you think the client is expecting us to do?
- What do you think are the main issues we will have to address?
- What's the first step you think you need to take?
- How would you go about tackling x issue?
- [This] is going to be a big risk for the client, how might you handle it?

- How do you think the other side will react? What will they be looking for?
- How can we break this project down into key stages?
- How long do you think it will take?
- What timetable do you envisage?
- What resources will you need?
- How will you divide up the work between you/who will be best placed to do these tasks?
- How will you co-ordinate/communicate with …?
- How can you keep costs down?

By the end of the discussion the team should have a clear plan of action. As you have got them thinking for themselves right from the start, you will find that as the matter progresses, they continue to do so. Before coming to you to check how to proceed, they will start to think what the next steps might be and come with suggestions. If they don't and passively ask 'What do you want us to do next?', you need to persist with the coaching approach. Ask them:

- What have you considered so far?
- What are the advantages of doing that?
- What are the risks?
- How will the client or the other side react?

Using this brainstorming and coaching approach will encourage them to use their initiative rather than rely on you for all the answers. You will still need to supervise them and monitor their progress, but you will find you have to do less chasing. You will see your team learning and growing in confidence and for many leaders in law firms this is highly rewarding.

For those who are **experienced and know what to do**, there are three approaches you can take.

**1. Reassure:**

If they are **experienced but cautious, lacking confidence to act independently**, it is important that you reassure them. You might be tempted to ask them to just get on with it, but you need to build their confidence and wean them off your support. Ask them to create their own action plan to present to you. This forces them to draw on their experience while giving them (and you) a safety net in case they have got anything wrong or missed something. As they present the plan, try to avoid taking over: ask questions to get them to build on their thinking or correct it where required. Where they have come up with good ideas, praise them and show you are delighted they could do this without your help: this will build confidence. Ensure the plan includes interim check-ins where they come to you and report on progress and can run ideas past you if they need the reassurance that this is the best way to proceed.

**2. Motivate/sell:**
If they are experienced but may not prioritize the work (for example, because it is a non-fee earning project, or it is work for another team or jurisdiction where they have no relationship with the client), it is important that you motivate them. You will need to sell the value of the work and the benefits – to them and to others – and then ask them to put a plan together. You don't need to see a detailed plan, just an overview with the focus on deliverables and a timetable, including how they will report to you on progress. Asking for a plan gets them started, gives them ownership and by being forced to put a timetable together, it will push the work up their priority list. If this fails, you will have to negotiate with them and monitor progress more closely.

**3. Delegate and let go:**
If they are **experienced and you can trust them to get on with it**, you need to let go! You want to give them as much autonomy as you can to decide how they will complete the work. Let them create the action plan of who is going to do what, when, the resources they will need and how they will report on progress. This saves you time, gives them ownership and the satisfaction of knowing that you trust them to do a great job.

Often you may be working with a team with different levels of experience. In this case, rely on the more experienced team members to put the plan together but ensure that those with less experience have the clarity they need for their tasks. This often means you need to encourage your experienced members to use the right supervision approach when they are delegating to less experienced team members.

## Apply: *Clarify how* planner

Still thinking about your project, start by identifying the supervision approach you should use to ***clarify how*** the work should be done.

| **Inexperienced** | | **Experienced** | | |
|---|---|---|---|---|
| **Train/tell (sat nav)** | **Brainstorm and coach** | **Reassure** | **Motivate/sell** | **Delegate and let go** |
| Use for novices, when they don't know where or how to start. | Use for keen learners who have a little experience on which to build. | Use for cautious intermediates. You can trust them to know what to do, but they lack confidence to act independently. | Use for jaded experts or those juggling conflicting priorities. They know what to do but you can't trust them to get it done on time or to the standard required. | Use for self-reliant experts. You can trust them as they are experienced, confident and motivated to get it done. |
| Maximum supervision | | ⟷ | | Minimum supervision |
| Minimum autonomy | | | | Maximum autonomy |

Once you have selected the right supervision approach for your project, plan what you will say or ask to create the plan with them or what you will check if the team is creating the plan themselves.

| ***Clarify how:*** | **What you will say/ask/check:** |
|---|---|
| 1. Steps to take to complete the work | |
| 2. Timetable and milestones | |
| 3. Budget/resources | |

| 4. Roles and responsibilities | |
|---|---|
| 5. How decisions will be made | |
| 6. How team members will communicate with each other and other stakeholders | |
| 7. How to meet quality standards | |

**Now review your *Clarify how* plan – does the approach mean:**

- ✓ You and the team will have a common understanding of how they will deliver the project?
- ✓ It will make it easy for you to monitor the team's progress?
- ✓ The discussions to create or review the plan will give you greater confidence in the team's ability and drive to deliver the results?
- ✓ Your chosen approach will demonstrate appropriate levels of trust in or support for the team?
- ✓ Your chosen approach will motivate the team and give them confidence to proceed?

# Chapter 4

# Difficulties to avoid

## Why

The team are now ready to get going on the work. The **D** is a double check to make sure you have considered any ***Difficulties*** which might lie ahead so that you plan how to avoid them – and ensure they are included in the action plan.

This is particularly important for optimists – who tend to overestimate the abilities of the team and underestimate the complexity of problems. Without anticipating problems, it becomes increasingly difficult to manage client or stakeholder expectations. These difficulties might be quite simple or straightforward and just require the team leader to think what could go wrong – to ask a few 'what if?' questions. What if:

- The project scope changes?
- The team meets unexpected obstacles?
- The fee estimate or budget is breached?
- The team lacks experience or expertise to solve a problem?
- A key member of the team is unavailable or sick?
- Other work takes a higher priority?
- The client or other side is slow in providing input?
- The team meets resistance to what it is trying to do?

Asking a few 'what if?' questions helps you to identify where your team may need your support and helps you prepare contingency plans or take preventative action. If you are an optimist, this ensures you avoid any nasty surprises.

Alternatively, if you are a pessimist you may have a tendency to focus on such difficulties without prompting. If so, this stage is about getting some balance: recognizing the difficulties and at the same time showing your team that it is possible to work around them.

I coached a practice group leader who had taken over a team following the departure of a more senior partner to a competitor, taking many clients with her. The new leader could only see the current situation as a problem and spoke to the team in very negative terms about the difficulties ahead, how much they were expecting of everyone and how they would all need to work really hard to rebuild the practice. When discussing this, everything they said was delivered quietly and with a big sigh. They felt hugely responsible for the security of employment for those remaining in the team and the road ahead appeared very challenging. I didn't doubt that they were doing everything they could to help the team survive, but their negative style unsettled the team even further. They undermined the team's confidence and very soon further departures followed. People don't want to belong to a negative team. They want to have confidence that a leader can see the problem yet has a plan to lead them through the difficulties – it needs to be more than 'try harder'.

This group leader was one of the people I came across that really clarified the need to adopt the **ABCDE** approach. They were stuck deep in **D** – in a valley of despair, focusing on all the difficulties facing the team. This was not impactful leadership – all they were doing was making the team members more anxious. No one could see the direction of travel – all they heard was that it was going to be hard. They needed to tell the team clearly what they had to achieve (**A**) together and how they would all personally benefit from the hard work of rebuilding the practice (**B**). They also needed to discuss plans for how to do this (**C**). We designed a retreat where the leader could set direction, enthuse the team and then spend time in a series of mini workshops to clarify the steps to take. It was a successful event and the team then rallied around.

## How

Difficulties come in two main forms – ***risks*** to the project and ***resistance*** from people who don't support or even want to block what you are doing. These are dealt with separately but of course there can be some overlap.

### How to plan for risks

Team leaders with project management experience will be used to identifying risks and planning how to handle them should they arise. Risk can come in a range of forms:

- Timing e.g. a deadline is missed, bottlenecks in work flow, the impact of a project which drags on
- Staffing/resourcing e.g. key team members or experts are unavailable or absent, teams are too busy to juggle multiple projects
- Financial e.g. fees exceed the estimate or cap, the budget is breached, out of scope work requires additional time
- Dissatisfied clients/damaged relationships e.g. the work product or service does not meet expectations
- Commercial e.g. loss of market share, loss of key client or loss of firm's experts to a competitor
- Reputation and liability e.g. poor advice, errors, missed deadlines/court dates.

How you handle risks will depend on the probability of them happening and the seriousness of the impact on what you are trying to achieve. Risk management can be complex but a basic approach is to decide whether to:

- **Accept** the risk, making a decision that this is commercial or economic e.g. accepting the need to provide a fixed fee otherwise you will not get the work
- **Avoid** a risk by changing the project or scope or even deciding not to go ahead e.g. telling the client you will not proceed unless the timetable is adjusted
- **Reduce** the probability that the risk will occur or reduce the impact if it does, through contingency planning e.g. having an agreed protocol for managing out of scope work
- **Share** the risk with other stakeholders e.g. the client or through insurance.

## Apply: *Difficulties* planner (managing risks)

Thinking of your project, complete the following table to identify risks, the impact they might have and how you will manage them.

| **Identify possible risks** | What is the **probability** that the risk will occur? Is it: *High/medium/ low* | What is the **impact** if the risk occurs? Is it: *High/medium/ low* | Plan how to **manage** significant risks. Will you: *Accept/avoid/ reduce/share* |
|---|---|---|---|
| 1. Timing (deadlines, bottlenecks, matter dragging on) | | | |
| 2. Staffing/resourcing | | | |
| 3. Financial (fees exceed estimate, out of scope work) | | | |
| 4. Dissatisfied clients/damaged relationships | | | |
| 5. Commercial (e.g. loss of market share/loss of key clients/loss of experts to competitor) | | | |
| 6. Reputational/liability (poor advice, missed deadlines) | | | |

## How to overcome resistance from people

On internal projects, often the biggest risk your team faces is resistance from people affected by what you are trying to do. If a project introduces some form of change, there will always be winners and losers. Even a project which focuses on improving the way things are done and looks like it will be welcomed by all can meet resistance. Some people just don't like change and don't want to have to change their routines. These people may fail to embrace the new approach or provide input to the project when asked. Others may more actively resist what the team is doing because they disagree with the aims or because even though the firm may win, they perceive that they personally will lose out.

> One Business Development department I worked with introduced client relationship management software which was meant to make it easier to collaborate over clients by capturing and sharing data. Most partners could see the gains that this would bring, but others felt threatened and became territorial over their relationships. They refused to share information about their clients or contacts as they didn't want to dilute their own influence or opportunities with them. Their resistance derailed the project for months.

Anticipating who will win and who will lose out before the project starts helps us identify how to make winners' support more visible and how to minimize the roadblocks or obstacles that those who stand to lose out might put in the way of the project's success.

To plan for resistance, you need to think about the different stakeholders in the project, how much impact they will have and whether you think they will actively support or undermine the team's efforts. The next table describes different levels of stakeholder support or resistance. If it is an important or powerful stakeholder then you need to plan action to mobilize their support or to neutralize their resistance.

**Passive** | **Active**

**Winners and those who support**

**Passive support: *'Let it happen'***

***Support is likely to be hidden:***
- Agreeing with you in private
- Not showing support in meetings
- Not volunteering ideas until requested
- May need chasing for input

***Action to take:***
1. Spend time on these people as they are easier to convert and their support may bring others along
2. Explore what is stopping them being more supportive; educate on the benefits
3. Invest time in building the relationship: involve them, encourage ideas and solutions
4. Try to make their support more public
5. Create quick wins to build confidence that the project/change will be successful

**Active support: *'Make it happen'***

***Support is visible and energetic:***
- Providing public support
- Praising the initiative
- Impatient for the project/change
- Volunteering ideas and time

***Action to take:***
1. Use as a champion and make their support visible to others
2. Ask them to influence others, use their own networks to widen support
3. Agree objectives to progress the project
4. Involve them in decision making
5. Delegate tasks and responsibilities

**Losers or those against**

**Passive resistance: *'Ignore it happening'***

***Resistance is likely to be covert:***
- Saying 'yes' and doing the opposite
- Prioritizing other things
- Hinting that it won't work
- Forgetting to use the new approach/procedures

***Action to take:***
1. Provide a forum for exploring concerns and causes of resistance
2. Problem solve together
3. Find opportunities to build common ground
4. Praise behaviours that are supportive of the project/change

**Active resistance: *'Stop it happening'***

***Resistance is likely to be overt:***
- Saying 'no'
- Challenging, arguing, disagreeing, ridiculing
- Trying to undermine you, your project or those involved
- Debating your approach

***Action to take:***
1. Don't ignore, discuss in private and ask questions to understand their perspective
2. Acknowledge their value or contribution elsewhere

**Passive** | **Active**

| 5. Be specific about any blocking behaviours and explain impact on the project/change/them<br>6. Monitor | 3. Handle objections and provide rationale and evidence for decisions, but avoid a hard sales approach or coercion<br>4. Negotiate and be prepared to settle for them letting you get on with it; you may never win their full support<br>5. Monitor |
|---|---|
| **Passive** | **Active** |

## Apply: *Difficulties* planner (overcoming resistance)

Thinking of your project, start by putting the names of key stakeholders in the following table. To do this:

1. First consider the stakeholder's level of support for the project (vertical axis): are they strongly against the project (resistant) or highly supportive of the project?
2. Now consider how actively the stakeholder will help or hinder the project (horizontal axis): will they be passive and less likely to demonstrate their support or resistance or active and more likely to act or their support or resistance?

Once you have assessed their level of support and how passive/active, map their position on the table and insert their name. Then plan the action you and the team will need to take to mobilize their support or neutralize their resistance (see the tips in the previous table).

| | **Passive support:** ***'Let it happen'*** | **Active support:** ***'Make it happen'*** |
|---|---|---|
| **Supportive of the project** | What action can you take with these stakeholders to make their support more visible i.e. move them into 'make it happen'? | How can you focus their support to win others over or help you deliver the project? |
| | **Passive:** less likely to demonstrate their support or resistance | **Active**: more likely to act on their support or resistance |

| | **Passive resistance: *'Ignore it happening'*** | **Active resistance: *'Stop it happening'*** |
|---|---|---|
| **Against the project** | What action can you take with these stakeholders to win them over enough to at least move them to 'let it happen'? | Plan how to neutralize their objections – it may be sufficient to just move them to 'ignore it'. |
| | **Passive:** less likely to demonstrate their support or resistance | **Active**: more likely to act on their support or resistance |

**Now review your *Difficulties* plan (for both risk and resistance):**

- Have you thought of both short-term and longer-term difficulties?
- If you ran the project plans past someone who is less enthusiastic, would they identify additional risks or resistance?
- Are your plans for overcoming any risks specific?
- Will it be easy for you to monitor and report on how risks are being managed?
- Will your plans for communicating with stakeholders address any resistance and make support more visible?
- What quick wins will you be able to achieve to win more support?

# Chapter 5

# Evaluate

## Why

The final stage is an enthusiastic summary supplemented with plans for how you will monitor progress and assess the success of the project. 'What gets measured, gets done' is a common saying and we do feel more accountable if we need to report on progress to someone else, whether it is a personal goal such as getting fit or whether a work goal. In the absence of monitoring and evaluation, a project team can sense that the leader is not really interested in the pace of the project progressing and so things can drift.

Agreeing how often and in what ways you will monitor progress, report to stakeholders and finally how you will assess the project outcomes, keeps everyone focused especially if you have team members working on multiple projects.

I have attended far too many meetings where everyone has discussed and agreed a new idea, but there has been limited accountability for implementation and no follow-up to monitor who has completed actions or who is struggling to do so. Those who have succeeded need to be congratulated. Recognition is a key motivator for many of us. If we feel our contribution is not noticed there is a tendency to focus our efforts where they will be appreciated. If someone is failing to progress their actions, this must not be ignored. They may need more support – what are the obstacles and how can they be overcome? Or, it may be that the failure to progress is an indicator of a bigger problem for the project which means the plans need to be reviewed.

Monitoring progress against the timetable and budget means that you can quickly spot problems and manage stakeholder expectations.

To boost the morale of the team it is good to have some early opportunities for a sense of achievement. For stakeholders, an early sign of success or a quick win helps to win more support, maintains interest in the project and builds confidence that the team will deliver. Piloting a new approach and getting a quick win in one area can create the momentum for change across the wider firm.

Finally, having plans for how the project outcomes will be evaluated is critical for keeping focus throughout.

On one leadership programme, we set quantifiable objectives for improving communication in the leaders' teams based on results from an engagement survey. The survey identified specific behaviours that needed to change to overcome the power of the grapevine. The development programme helped the leaders explore and practise the changes they would need to make to meet the target improvement in scores – for example, holding regular team meetings. The follow-up survey showed significant improvement in team members' motivation, that key information was being shared more promptly and reliance on the grapevine had significantly reduced. This reinforced the benefits of investing time in team meetings. It also pinpointed a couple of teams where insufficient progress had been made and enabled targeted support to be provided there. Without this measurement, I am convinced the busy team leaders would not have prioritized team meetings in the same way.

## How

There are a range of ways to measure and report on progress and to evaluate outcomes. These, of course, all rely on you being clear on what you are trying to achieve at the outset. Remember, a good ***Achieve*** statement will include tangible indicators of success.

To monitor progress towards the final goal, you need to break the project down into key stages and plan measures of success for each stage – these could be in relation to activities, management of issues or risks, the timetable, fees/budget, client relationship, etc.

You then need to consider who needs to know about this progress. Identify the key stakeholder groups, internal and external, and for each group you need to identify:

- How regularly you need to report: this could be daily, weekly, monthly, at key milestones
- The format which would be most helpful. This could be a regular email, call, meeting or status report or it could be by providing a visual tracker such as a RAG report (red, amber, green)
- The focus and level of detail for monitoring: activities/issues and risks/timetable/fees etc.

On longer projects, it is very helpful to have evaluation points at the end of key stages in which the team can review:

- What is going well
- What is not going as well as expected
- What changes to make for the next stage of the project.

These reviews need not take much time. In 15–30 minutes, a team can identify specific lessons learned to make the next stage of the project more efficient and effective. Keep the review informal so that team members feel more comfortable voicing their views. I favour standing around a flipchart and brainstorming ideas, rather than sitting around a table. The pace and energy levels are higher as people are on their feet, there is less eye contact and so it is easier for more junior people to contribute ideas and they may have the key to why something is or is not working.

At the end of the project, it is important to complete a proper review to assess how well the outcomes were achieved and what can be learned to make your team more competitive.

1. Were the objectives met?
2. Were the anticipated benefits realized?
3. How profitable was the project/did the project provide good return on the time and resources invested?
4. What could have been done better, faster or more cheaply?
5. How else could the team work more efficiently on a similar project?
6. How could communication be improved?

7. How satisfied was the client and how could client satisfaction be improved?
8. What was the impact on the reputation and skills of the team and individuals?
9. What would make it more rewarding or satisfying to work on a similar project in the future?
10. What know how was generated and how will this be circulated?

To do this evaluation, you can have a team review and a client/stakeholder review so that you get the different perspectives. It might be in the form of a meeting or a survey. Keeping the tone informal is usually best for encouraging feedback and it is critical as leader not to react defensively to any feedback that things could be improved. If there is criticism, encourage the team to be constructive and propose solutions – 'How would you change that?', 'What do you want to see happening next time?', etc. For very high-profile projects or ones which have proved exceptionally difficult, it can be helpful to have an independent colleague run the review on your behalf. For example, in larger firms someone in the business development team might be able to elicit more insightful feedback than the partner who ran the project.

## Apply: *Evaluate* planner

Thinking of your project, start by identifying how you will evaluate and report on the progress of your team's work i.e. for regular reporting.

| **Regular reporting planner** | | | |
|---|---|---|---|
| **Who – key stakeholders for regular reporting:** | **When – frequency of reporting:**<br>• Daily<br>• Weekly<br>• Fortnightly<br>• Monthly<br>• At end of stage | **How – most appropriate format of status report:**<br>• Email<br>• Call<br>• Meeting<br>• Tracker | **Focus of report – progress on:**<br>• Activities<br>• Issues/risks<br>• Timetable<br>• Financials |
| **Core team** | | | |

| Regular reporting planner | | | |
|---|---|---|---|
| **Who – key stakeholders for regular reporting:** | **When – frequency of reporting:**<br>• Daily<br>• Weekly<br>• Fortnightly<br>• Monthly<br>• At end of stage | **How – most appropriate format of status report:**<br>• Email<br>• Call<br>• Meeting<br>• Tracker | **Focus of report – progress on:**<br>• Activities<br>• Issues/risks<br>• Timetable<br>• Financials |
| **Extended team** | | | |
| **Client** | | | |
| **Internal management** | | | |

Next consider how you will review success at the end of stage and end of project to learn lessons for the next stage or the next project.

| | Lessons learned planner | | |
|---|---|---|---|
| | **Who to involve:**<br>*Team/client/other stakeholders* | **Format:**<br>*Call/meeting/ survey/facilitated meeting or workshop* | **Questions to ask to learn lessons for the next stage of the project or for other projects:**<br>*Objectives met/benefits/financials/ team efficiency/communication/client satisfaction/know how and learning* |
| **End of stage** | | | |

| | Lessons learned planner | | |
|---|---|---|---|
| | **Who to involve:** *Team/client/other stakeholders* | **Format:** *Call/meeting/ survey/facilitated meeting or workshop* | **Questions to ask to learn lessons for the next stage of the project or for other projects:** *Objectives met/benefits/financials/ team efficiency/communication/client satisfaction/know how and learning* |
| **End of project** | | | |

**Now review your *Evaluate* plans – will they:**

- ✓ Help you motivate the team and ensure they focus effort on the right things?
- ✓ Be feasible when you are busy/working on multiple projects?
- ✓ Make it easy to delegate some of the monitoring?
- ✓ Enhance client satisfaction?
- ✓ Ensure lessons learned will help the team deliver even better results next time?

# Summary: Part 1

## Key takeaways:

- The **ABCDE** tool helps you to communicate efficiently with your team so together you can deliver great results.
- It is rare for a team leader to instinctively cover all the five elements in the **ABCDE** tool simply because different personality preferences make these steps more or less comfortable.
- Set direction for your team by telling them what they need to ***Achieve***.
- Keep your ***Achieve*** statements short, specific, positive and focused on outcomes.
- Enthuse and motivate your team by explaining the ***Benefits*** of what they are doing for stakeholders and for them personally.
- Use the 'so what that means for you' bridging phrase to make a powerful case by linking it to something of value to them.
- Ensure you support your team by ***Clarifying how*** the work will be done including scope of work, timetable, roles and responsibilities, communication and decision-making protocols, resource and budget plans.
- Vary the amount of instruction and supervision you provide based on the team's experience, motivation and confidence to act independently.
- Help your team anticipate and plan how to overcome ***Difficulties*** – whether in the shape of risks or resistance.
- For risks decide how to handle them based on the nature of the risk, its probability and impact: can you accept the risk, avoid it, reduce it or share it?
- Plan stakeholder communications to make support for your project visible and to reassure or neutralize those who may have concerns or objections.
- Keep your team on track by agreeing how you will ***Evaluate*** progress and monitor outcomes.

- At the outset plan for regular reporting and for end of project evaluations so you learn lessons for the next project.
- A collection of the planning exercises is provide in Appendix 2 so that you can use them whenever you are planning a project or an initiative.

## Coming up

**A**: In Part 2 we help you identify your leadership style, based on behavioural preferences.

**B**: Being aware of your leadership style helps you understand how others may perceive you and how to adjust your style to get the best results.

**C**: We will look at four main leadership styles and then several hybrid styles. Hybrid styles combine two or three styles which are common amongst lawyers. If you have already taken a DISC, Insights Discovery® or Social Styles behavioural assessment you will be able to link your results to the case studies and tips on adjusting your style.

**D**: As you read you should be able to identify your own style but if you are still not sure by the end of Part 2, there are a couple of summary pages to help you pin it down. An alternative is to take an assessment and there are links for this in Appendix 1.

**E**: By the end of Part 2 you should have a clear idea of small changes you can make to be an even more effective leader.

# Part 2

# Your leadership style

# Introduction

Your leadership reputation is based on how people experience you – what they see you do; what they hear you say; how you make them feel. It is not based on your intentions – however valid they might be. For example, one partner was convinced that his team needed to compete on quality, so he tried to review everything before it went out, even from senior associates. His behaviour created bottlenecks and stress for everyone. He made the team feel that they weren't good enough, not to be trusted. Another partner wanted to protect her under-resourced team. She did all the business development for the team as she didn't want to ask them to take on more tasks on top of fee earning. In some 360 feedback she was devastated to find that the team resented this – they felt excluded. Another leader feared for his team who were not meeting their targets as markets were difficult at that time and he thought they were too laid back about it. He kept telling them how difficult things were, hoping to spur them into action, but he made them feel insecure and that they were imminently going to be made redundant.

All their intentions were good but just not executed in the right way to make the team members feel good about their contribution, their role and their future in their team. All these leaders needed to be a little more self-aware about how their behaviours would be interpreted by their teams.

This is where understanding your behavioural preferences which create your leadership style can be so helpful. It is an insight into how others might perceive you.

You may think that you are:

- Demanding but team members may experience this as coercive or controlling
- Collegiate but others may think you are too friendly
- Focused on high standards but others may experience you as fussy
- Authoritative but others may find you aloof.

Think about this for your own style.

| Write down five words or short phrases to describe the type of leader you try to be. | Now, list five words or short phrases that a team might use to describe you if you weren't in the room. |
|---|---|
| 1. | 1. |
| 2. | 2. |
| 3. | 3. |
| 4. | 4. |
| 5. | 5. |

## Behavioural preferences

The best way to think about behavioural preferences is to think about what feels most comfortable to you. We make choices all the time at work. For example, if someone has done some work for you and gets it completely wrong:

- you could choose to go and yell at them – not very effective but it happens
- you could choose to talk them through all the changes that need to be made
- you could choose to mark up the changes or
- you could re-do the work yourself and decide never to trust that person again.

Also, think about how you raise your profile in the market – do you feel most comfortable:

- networking
- writing articles
- running a seminar or
- holding a sporting event?

Each of these approaches has different merits, but most lawyers will feel more comfortable and enthusiastic about some than others.

There are a whole range of tools for diagnosing your behavioural style. Some are more complex and go deeper than others. In this book I am focusing on simple profiling tools that look at key preferences and are summarized in four quadrant models: DISC, Insights Discovery® and Social Styles.[9] They do not assess your intelligence, your values, your skills or experience – just how you prefer to do things. They are easy and quick to understand and sufficient for looking at how the preferences affect the way you lead.

These behaviour profiling tools look at whether you tend to be more:

- Outspoken or reserved
- Quick to respond or considered
- Task or people focused
- Critical or accepting.

The resulting feedback provides insights on:

- What motivates you, what you will prioritize and what you try to avoid
- How you like to communicate and influence others
- What you are likely to do well and what you are likely to find more challenging
- How others might perceive you.

## Leadership styles

Of course, people are complex and these profiling tools are blunt – but they do give insights into why people behave and react differently, why they lead differently or want to be led differently. Once aware of these differences it helps you to adjust your own style to be more effective when leading people, especially if they have a different style to you. This is covered in Part 3 of the book.

Most of the leaders I coach who are having problems with a team member, boss or client find that the person they perceived to be

---

[9] Some law firms favour other diagnostic tools such as MBTI, 16PF or Hogan Development Survey. These are all good and valid (I use them in my coaching too) but they result in more complex findings and are not so easy to map against the **ABCDE** model.

'difficult' is just someone with a different style who needs to be managed or related to in a different way. For example, a team leader who is very optimistic and enthusiastic could clash with a team member who is sceptical and wants proof that the team leader's approach isn't risky.

With a good understanding of your underlying preferences it is easier to develop and enhance the skills and behaviours you need as a leader – with your team, colleagues and your clients.

## The four main leadership styles

We will start with a description of four leadership styles based on four preferred approaches to leading, each with their own merits:

- Results-Driven
- Relationship-Focused
- Security-Oriented
- Risk-Averse.

They are set out in a four quadrant model as follows, showing the underlying preferences:

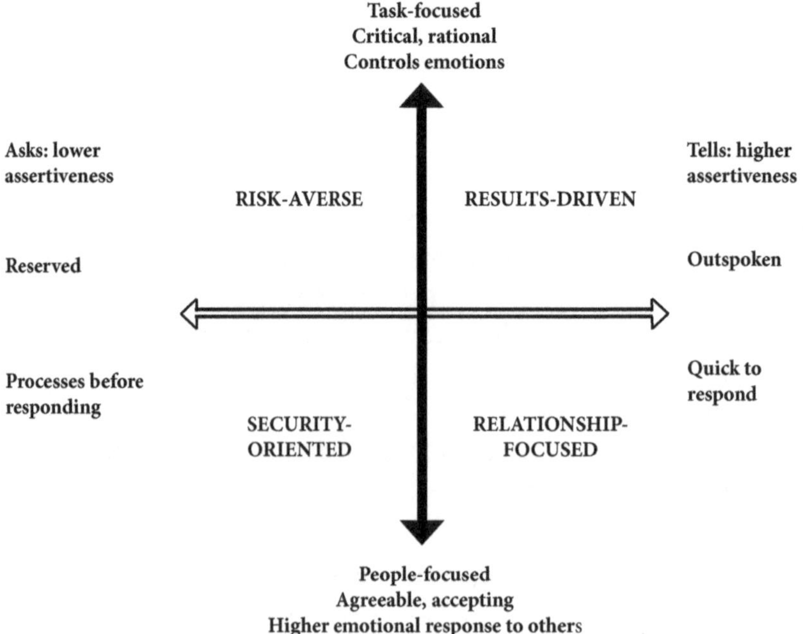

In these four main leadership styles, each leader has a very strong single preference to use that style: they behave consistently in this way. You might be like one of these. However, many people have one stronger preference backed up by one other or even two other preferences. The stronger preference is likely to be what your teams will see you do most often, what they see you rely on to get things done at work.

The chapters on each of the four leadership styles include examples of how this can play out in a law firm, an explanation of the style and how such a leader could use the **ABCDE** approach to be more effective. See if you identify with them or if any of the five words you listed earlier to describe the leader you try to be, match. If not, perhaps you recognize other leaders like this.

## Hybrid styles

After describing the four main leadership styles, in the following chapter we will look at some common hybrid styles in law firms – these are combinations of two or three of the styles of almost equal strength which I come across frequently in my work with lawyers.

I have undertaken thousands of psychometric profiles for lawyers, and the majority have two and sometimes three equally strong preferred ways of working. The blend creates some great strengths and makes the lawyer more flexible in their approach. Often these double or triple strengths get them promoted to leadership roles. However, when leading, these strengths can sometimes become traps too. For example:

- A lawyer who did well because they were fast paced and could fix problems quickly can become a leader who gets exhausted trying to fix all the problems around them.
- A lawyer who has a strong service orientation and bends over backwards to avoid confrontation may not be sufficiently demanding or assertive with their team.
- A lawyer that is highly results and task focused may find it challenging to invest time in motivating and developing a team.

When I coach lawyers, I often find we can use their strengths combined with the **ABCDE** approach to help them prioritize things that they would ignore when busy or just not think worthwhile. For example, a detail-oriented leader who also likes routine can adopt a *new* routine to ensure they focus first on the bigger picture and what needs to be achieved (**A**) when talking to their team.

You may have come across examples like these hybrid leaders and have your own ideas about what you would like that leader to do to be more effective. For each, I have added a few tips that I find help them to get better results when leading others. If you think you are like one of the hybrid leaders, I hope the tips will help you too.

Of course, it is also important to remember that you may have learned to adjust your style already as your career has progressed. For example, you might be a very talkative leader who has learned the hard way that you need to listen more to your team – but that preference is still likely to be there to talk rather than listen. Alternatively, you might be a big picture thinker who has learned the need to focus on details, but you are still happiest when able to think strategically. We can operate outside our comfort zone in this way, but it takes more focus and energy. If we are forced to do so all the time, there is a risk that we will find the job dissatisfying or even burn out. That's why it is so effective if you can find a niche in which you can make the most of your preferences and only have to make small adjustments to be effective – as described in this book. An awareness of your preferences can also help you recruit people to your team who complement your style and who enjoy doing the things you dislike doing.

## Do you already know your preferred style?

These four main leadership styles are compatible with the DISC, Insights Discovery® and Social Styles profiling tools used in many law firms. These are indicated in the following table so if you have already completed such a profiling assessment you can quickly turn to the relevant style or styles for you.

| **Profiling tool** | **Results-Driven** | **Relationship-Focused** | **Security-Oriented** | **Risk-Averse** |
|---|---|---|---|---|
| DISC | Dominance | Influence | Steadiness | Compliance |
| Insights Discovery® | Fiery Red | Sunshine Yellow | Earth Green | Cool Blue |
| Social Styles | Driver | Expressive | Amiable | Analyser |

If you haven't had the opportunity to complete a profiling tool you can do so easily – turn to Appendix 1 for more information and links to test publishers. Some are free to take, for others there will be a charge.

However, I hope the description of each style and the ten questions under 'Does this sound like you?' will help you to identify your own style and how to adjust it without the need for an assessment. Before progressing to the hybrid leadership styles, Chapter 10 provides a summary table of all these questions to help you identify your own preferred style/s.

# Chapter 6

# Results-Driven leaders

This style is compatible with a preference for Dominance in DISC, the Fiery Red in Insights Discovery® and the Driver in Social Styles.

## Meet Aza

Aza is a leader of a large practice group with a very driven, competitive style. Aza focuses relentlessly on key projects to change the market perception of the practice so that it is seen as modern and commercial through use of technology and competitive pricing.

Aza is a big picture thinker and relies on a few people to implement the vision. This trusted group picks up an idea quickly and makes it happen, pushing through barriers and doing the follow-through. This approach in the short term frees up Aza to keep moving forwards, building success upon success.

However, it also means Aza sometimes works around senior people who should have been involved. Aza is clear, decisive and direct about what is wanted but doesn't have time for people who don't get on board or for those who are negative or question the direction taken. If they encounter resistance, they will either confront it directly and talk the partner round or just ignore anyone not sufficiently influential.

Associates respect Aza but some find their hands-off style challenging. Aza is demanding, gives opportunities to those who appear ambitious and confident; they seek out those with a can-do attitude and who will take the initiative.

However, Aza's run of successes eventually stalled. They had achieved much but in the end this Results-Driven style failed because they alienated too many people in the practice and firm. When it came to selling the vision of an ambitious bolt-on for the practice, Aza was braver than most of the partners and failed to listen to their concerns or get the full backing of the board. Frustrated at the stagnation, Aza left the firm.

Six months later I catch up with Aza at their new firm. They admit that it took this failure to really appreciate the need to listen and consult in the way we had discussed before. Aza is now ready to adjust to a more collaborative leadership style. It is hard work going against ingrained behaviours, but slowly they make progress, consulting more widely, spending time influencing others. They are surprised to find this approach makes it easier to deliver results than before.

## How Results-Driven are you?

Every leader is likely to describe themselves as Results-Driven, especially working in a law firm where getting a result for a client is what matters whether completing a deal, delivering a project, finalizing a contract or winning a case.

However, in workshops I find that when asked what type of leader people aim to be, most lawyers don't describe themselves in words associated with Results-Driven leadership. In my experience of working with lawyers only a small proportion have this as their preferred approach. This is probably because being Results-Driven doesn't sit well with the collaborative nature of partnership or the detailed work required of lawyers in the early years. It now also takes too long to get to be a partner or in a position of power for many young Results-Driven lawyers – they seek careers which are more entrepreneurial or with more instant results.

Some lawyers are very disappointed to discover when they complete a personality profile that they are not Results-Driven. However, the more they argue the case, the more they often illustrate other personality preferences! It is important to recognize that you can be a fantastic lawyer and a great leader, without being primarily Results-Driven. Keep an open mind.

Truly Results-Driven leaders put action first, they push themselves and like to drive others. They focus on profits and like to win at all costs. They are unafraid of conflict. They love a challenge, hate failure and this competitiveness means that they can achieve great things with their teams, as long as they can carry their teams along with them. If not, they end up as frustrated solo-practitioners and can drive themselves into the ground.

When communicating with their teams, Results-Driven leaders tend to focus on the goal, what they want the team to achieve. However, they may be so impatient to get the result that they decide not to include others whom they perceive to be too slow. This means they sometimes struggle to delegate effectively at the senior associate stage – only delegating very basic tasks and dumping things on people at the last minute when they have run out of time to do it all themselves. Their hands-off style and lack of follow-through can sometimes leave team members struggling.

When leading they tend to have a very directive, decisive style: 'Do it because I'm telling you to do it.' Whilst this direction is good, an unaware team leader may become too autocratic or even coercive to get the best out of the team in the long run. Teams may complain that the style is not inclusive and their input is not valued.

In large law firms where people are more specialized, you often find lawyers with strong results-drive in areas such as private equity, banking and finance and restructuring – they relish the demanding clients and the challenge of aggressive timetables.

All styles are necessary for a healthy team and firm. The Results-Driven leader's biggest value is this drive for results, even in the face of opposition and difficult circumstances. In our **ABCDE** of leadership, they naturally focus on **A** – ***Achieve***. Their challenge is to be more patient and understanding of others – they need to supplement their style by thinking about using ***Benefits*** to enthuse people to work towards the result needed (the **B**) and by focusing on implementation (the **C**, **D** and **E**).

## Does this sound like you?

1. Are you driven and goal oriented?
2. Do you have a high need to achieve?
3. Are you more focused on results than people?
4. Do you like to have power and to exert control?

5. Are you direct and assertive in your communications?
6. Do you initiate? Are you a self-starter?
7. Can you be impatient and demanding?
8. Are you forceful and competitive?
9. Are you unafraid of conflict?
10. Do you relish a good argument to get to a better solution?

Many lawyers don't have this as their preferred style. They want to achieve, but success for them is defined by other criteria. In my experience of working with lawyers, it occurs more often as a back-up preference. If it feels partly right, that might be the case for you and you'll see it in two of the common hybrid styles. Consider whether the next style is more like you.

# Chapter 7

# Relationship-Focused leaders

This style is compatible with a preference for Influence in DISC, Sunshine Yellow in Insights Discovery® and the Expressive in Social Styles.

## Meet Bellamy

Bellamy is a new partner full of enthusiasm and energy with a great client portfolio which was the basis of their business case for partnership. These were relationships they had nurtured for years and were now coming to fruition with good quality and sizeable instructions for the team.

Bellamy enjoys meeting people and is a natural at networking. They have forged good connections across the market – some of these are more useful than others but Bellamy says you have to kiss a lot of frogs. They are collaborative and happy to cross-sell other partners – but insist on being kept closely involved so that clients don't feel neglected.

The team is very loyal, many are former trainees. Bellamy is fun to work with, spends time explaining legal issues so associates learn fast and helps them to raise their profile. As a rule, they always take a team member to any client meeting, even if the time can't be charged, as they believe interacting with clients is so critical for a successful career.

The downside of being in the team is that Bellamy is often too optimistic about deadlines and fees and doesn't push back against unreasonable client expectations. This can result in late nights and time being written-off, especially as much of their work is for fixed fees.

Now with a partner hourly rate this is becoming a problem and Bellamy needs to find ways of working more efficiently so that it is more profitable. They also need to tackle an associate who has hit a plateau and is just not using the initiative expected for the next level. Having been friends for years, Bellamy is reluctant to give the difficult feedback that unless things change the associate will not be promoted. The associate's cautious approach is starting to be a further drain on the profitability of the work.

The situation is creating stress and when stressed, Bellamy starts to talk without a filter – sharing too much information about the problems of working with fixed fees and a lack of confidence in the firm's management.

The Finance and HR Directors are concerned that Bellamy is not dealing well with the new responsibilities of partnership and I am asked to help. I encourage Bellamy to pause and plan – to develop more emotional control, to tackle problems in the team and to be more bullish with clients about fees. Bellamy retains an engaging style but becomes more direct and authoritative.

## How Relationship-Focused are you?

Are you the type of leader who puts relationships with clients and the team first? Most people like to be liked, but for Relationship-Focused leaders this is the primary motivator. One group leader told me he would rather fail, than succeed and not be liked.

Many lawyers have some degree of relationship-focus in their style because they are in a service industry. If this is not natural, they have learned to develop it. Truly Relationship-Focused leaders put people first and so describe their leadership style in people terms – they see themselves as team builders, mentors and enthusiasts who inspire others. They often get involved in recruitment and training too since they will tell you that people are the life-blood of the firm.

Leaders who prioritize relationships tend to be very communicative with their teams. They will make time for meetings and will want to involve the team in decisions. They will be positive and friendly and try to persuade someone to do something rather than tell them directly. They like to sell their ideas.

The stronger the preference to build relationships, the more outgoing and verbal they tend to be – they can talk to excess. Sometimes this style can be experienced as too enthusiastic for sceptical lawyers and with too much time spent talking, until a looming deadline creates the focus to get things done.

Leaders strongly motivated by relationships can have difficulties with anything that feels like rejection. For example, they can take a lost pitch very personally: 'Why didn't they like me?' It is this fear that makes it hard for them to confront problems directly. They will justify it by saying 'I don't want to upset them' and their concern will be 'They might not like me if I tell them this.' Instead, they try to coach, encourage, cajole. An unaware Relationship-Focused leader can therefore develop a leadership style that is too friendly and positive and may be seen by others as not sufficiently demanding.

In large law firms where people are more specialized, you will find lawyers with this preference often in areas where there is a high level of client contact – for example real estate, corporate, employment, family.

Healthy firms need a range of styles and the Relationship-Focused leader's biggest value is in motivating others to achieve results. In our **ABCDE** of leadership, they naturally focus on **B** – selling the ***Benefits*** of the opportunity or of what needs to be done. Their challenge is to keep sight of the outcome that needs to be ***Achieved*** (**A**) and to temper their enthusiasm by being more probing and practical – they need to plan how to get it done by the deadline and for what could go wrong (**C, D** and **E**).

## Does this sound like you?

1. Do you prioritize relationships over results?
2. Do you have a high need to be liked?
3. Do you like to win people round?
4. Do you like to talk and persuade?
5. Do you like to do business in a friendly way?
6. Are you positive and enthusiastic?
7. Are you optimistic?
8. Are you sometimes concerned you are too trusting?
9. Do you postpone difficult conversations, hoping things will improve?

10. Do you over-use praise?

If you think you are more reserved and sceptical than this, that you like to probe and have the evidence before embarking on an initiative, it is likely that you will fit better with one of the other styles. If it is a little like you, then it might be a back-up preference. You'll see it in four of the hybrid styles in Chapter 11.

# Chapter 8

# Security-Oriented leaders

This style is compatible with a preference for Steadiness in DISC, Earth Green in Insights Discovery® and the Amiable in Social Styles.

## Meet Coron

Coron is a group leader who has built a very efficient and profitable practice based on most of the work being pushed down to a junior or paralegal level. They are very proud of the team's collegiate culture and specialized skills which means they are doing more complex work than would ordinarily be done at this level. The team has processes and templates making it easy for everyone to use a set approach and work efficiently. Efficiency is Coron's favourite word.

Over several years Coron has invested time in developing two senior associates so that they can each manage large teams of paralegals. This frees up partner time to focus on business development and to answer any complex questions. The team needs a big pipeline of work to stay profitable and they have found social media and intermediaries are the best sources of new work.

Coron's supportive style means they make time to solve problems, ensure performance reviews are fair and thorough and rarely ask people to work unreasonable hours. There are several part-time lawyers in the team (Coron is an advocate of work-life balance and wellbeing at board level). In engagement surveys, the team always has the highest scores.

However, the team is rather self-contained; this creates problems when the firm starts to revisit its strategy. Although profitable, the team is not seen as core to the business. Coron finds it increasingly difficult to get funding for specialized software improvements, to increase headcount and even the team's business development budget is reduced as the firm focuses its resources on core clients and the new sectors.

Coron starts to feel very isolated in the partnership and sees this change of approach as a slap in the face given all the hard work in building the practice. They complain to the management board. This creates the impression that Coron is not strategic and too inflexible about adapting to the new sector focus – which would be entirely possible with a few changes. Coron threatens to find a new home for the practice – which the board doesn't want. This is when I'm asked to help.

Through the coaching Coron starts to see that the situation has been created by not engaging with the changes in the firm and in the wider market too. They have been too focused on making the team the best in the firm rather than on making the firm the best it can be. They have not invested time in collaborating with other partners, in cross-selling or in firmwide initiatives. Moreover, they had tended to ignore and not participate in partnership debates about moving to a sector focus approach – seeing this as irrelevant to the practice without appreciating it could result in the team becoming peripheral. Once over the sense of injustice about the changes, Coron recognizes the need to adapt the practice to better fit with the firm's new sector focus and we spend time planning how to align the team to the new strategy.

## How Security-Oriented are you?

Are you the type of leader who likes to create harmonious and collaborative teams so that disruption is minimized? Do you spend much of your time helping them work efficiently and ensuring they do things in the right way? Do you create the steps they need to follow, the process, checklists? This focus on process comes from wanting to have some certainty and control over what is going to happen, when and how. It provides a sense of security and this is the primary motivator for this type of leader.

Among lawyers it is common to have some degree of this style and for a few it is their strongest preference. You will find Security-Oriented lawyers in all areas because they are persistent, reliable, dependable and like to craft specialist skills. Partners often describe them as a safe pair of hands. Since it is an amiable, non-aggressive style, it may seem surprising to find that many litigators have it as a preference: court process and deadlines give some certainty for those who like to know what is happening and when. Security-Oriented lawyers are also attracted to corporate and commercial roles, to regulatory areas, private client, family and I have yet to profile a pensions or securitization lawyer who doesn't have this preference in their style.

Leaders who like certainty and security tend to take a steady approach to leading. If untrained, they can be a bit laid back at first, reactive to what needs to be done rather than looking ahead and thinking what they should prioritize. I am no longer surprised when coaching inexperienced leaders with this style to find that they do not yet have a proper system for prioritizing leadership work and may not even have a to-do list. Their reliance on doing one thing at a time means they have to learn to juggle and focus on what is most important, not just most urgent.

However, one of their strengths is to develop structure, so once they get into the habit of managing others they learn to organize, co-ordinate and make use of processes to get people working efficiently. They develop routines and structures for leading. This could be the use of a whiteboard in their office for monitoring progress or action trackers or they might have regular update meetings and catch-ups.

As a leader they prefer to have scheduled meetings rather than people dropping by to ask questions when they are working on something else. However, they are good listeners and patient so will not demonstrate their frustration when interrupted. They pride themselves on being fair and even-tempered; if they are stressed, they are unlikely to show it. They often like to delegate to a select group of lawyers whom they find easy to work with and whom they trust. They build very loyal teams. This can sometimes limit their opportunities to delegate if those lawyers are already busy on other things.

Their style is reserved and so when communicating with their teams they will provide information on a need-to-know basis. When making decisions they are often consultative, trying to build consensus. With their peers and people they don't know, there is a tendency to listen first before sharing their own ideas.

Leaders with this style can find unexpected change uncomfortable if it is not under their control. This can make them slower to accept the need to change and they can be perceived as inflexible or too slow to innovate because of the desire to follow what they know works well. If unaware of this tendency they can appear to others as too protective of their team, of the status quo and not sufficiently focused on end results.

However, this inflexibility is also one of their strengths. Their biggest value in law firms is that they are practical and a stabilizing force – sometimes it is their questions such as 'How's this going to work in practice?' that make more impetuous leaders recognize that their ideas need more thought before implementation.

In our **ABCDE** of leadership, Security-Oriented leaders focus on **C** – ***Clarifying how*** things should be done. Their challenge is not to get lost in implementation and to keep focused on the end result that needs to be ***Achieved*** (**A**). They also need to ensure they motivate people by highlighting the ***Benefits*** (**B**), especially for anyone involved who is outside their immediate team. When it comes to (**D**) ***Difficulties***, they need to challenge themselves by checking whether the usual approach will be fit for purpose on this occasion and particularly to think about ways of doing things faster to keep costs down. For them ***Evaluating*** progress (**E**) is also key to keeping momentum and at the end a matter review can be a good routine to adopt so that they continuously improve their processes.

## Does this sound like you?

1. Are you consistent and persistent, working on things until they are finished?
2. Do you prefer to listen first before providing your input?
3. Are you at your most confident in familiar situations or with those you already know?
4. Are you patient and appear calm to others?
5. Do you like harmony and stability?

6. Do you see yourself as practical?
7. Do you like to focus on how things work and how things need to be done?
8. Do you like to have routines at work?
9. Do you have set ways of doing things?
10. Is one of your favourite sayings: 'If it's not broken, don't try to fix it?'

If this doesn't sound like you and you haven't yet strongly identified with the other styles described so far, then you might find that the next style is a better fit – it is very common among lawyers. The legal profession attracts them like a magnet. If it feels partly like you, it might be one of your back-up preferences and you'll see it occur in three of the hybrid styles in Chapter 11.

# Chapter 9

# Risk-Averse leaders

This style is compatible with a preference for Compliance in DISC, Cool Blue in Insights Discovery® and the Analyser in Social Styles.

## Meet Dana

Dana is a busy partner in a large practice group and has a formidable reputation as the go-to lawyer for complex issues. They are known as a thought leader and have an authoritative style which clients relish. They often complain about poor standards and the education of young lawyers and so run regular training sessions which are appreciated by the associates.

They believe the best way to develop a good legal brain is to force lawyers to think for themselves. When delegating they give plenty of freedom to do this at the start. In follow-up discussions they then quiz the associate and drill down into the detail. They demand perfect work product in content, style and presentation and at the review stage make many changes before work goes out the door. Once associates have worked for Dana for some time, they are familiar with how things should be phrased and presented, and so fewer changes need to be made. If an associate doesn't learn quickly, they are not used again.

Dana is formal when interacting with others and, being very task focused, doesn't like to waste time on chat. Occasionally they take associates out for a drink and then have a laugh together.

I get to meet Dana to help them respond to some upwards feedback. Although there are some very positive comments, others indicate they are too aloof, too demanding, and uncaring. Associates do not feel appreciated for their hard work and do not feel supported; more complex work could be delegated sooner and more help raising profile would be appreciated. This feedback also matches some given in exit interviews.

Our coaching discussion revealed that Dana thought it best to use only those associates you could trust so as to minimize supervision time. They thought praise was unnecessary and could undermine a focus on excellence. They were aghast to think that a partner should encourage and motivate associates – surely, they were being paid a good salary! They admitted to never having had a conversation with any of the associates about the type of work they wanted to do or their career aspirations.

However, Dana did genuinely care about the good associates. They thought about giving the right type of work to develop expertise and about ensuring the hours weren't excessive. Yet they had never explained this to them. They needed to learn to praise excellent work, to praise progress and to demonstrate appreciation. We turned these into leadership tasks to go on their to-do list. That way Dana remembered to praise, to give feedback about changes and to give more support when delegating to inexperienced lawyers. They also took each key associate out for lunch to talk about the work they liked and about their career aspirations. By the following year, the upward feedback had improved, and Dana was finding delegation more rewarding.

## How Risk-Averse are you?

Cautious, Risk-Averse leaders in law firms are focused on ensuring high standards are maintained and risks are minimized for their clients and for the firm. They take their leadership responsibilities seriously and like to have policies and best practice guidance for their teams to follow. Instead of directly saying, 'This is what I would like you to do', they tend to say, 'This is what the client expects' or 'This is what the firm expects'. They use rules to manage people. They have very high expectations of themselves and of others. They are naturally focused on problem solving and tend to approach leadership in the same way – as tasks to do and problems to solve. If things are going well, they tend to think not much is required of them and will prioritize fee earning work.

This style is analytical, logical, with a focus on avoiding error and is very common in lawyers. The lawyer is an attractive profession for people who like detail, facts and analysis. About 80% of the lawyers I have profiled have some degree of this in their style and many have it as their strongest preference, especially in areas where strong attention to detail is required throughout the career. Many tax lawyers have this as a very strong preference. Occasionally it is combined with a relationship-focus and hey presto you have your user-friendly tax lawyer who can explain complex schemes in a way that makes clients smile.

Often this Risk-Averse style is combined with some degree of security-orientation which can make it difficult to differentiate between the two styles, since we often experience them together. However, someone with this style is more concerned to get to the right answer and to avoid error, than to do things in a set way. We'll see more of this in the chapter on hybrid styles.

Leaders with this style try to avoid head-on conflict. When they are effective, they are clear with their teams about what is expected so that they pre-empt any difficult discussions when things don't meet their standards. Less experienced leaders may fall into the trap of not being clear upfront and then finding it difficult to give the feedback that this wasn't right. I have coached many Risk-Averse leaders who have experienced this problem and simply decided the lawyer wasn't up to their standards and so didn't use them again. This is not a good approach and you can only get away with it in large teams. Leaders with this style need to learn to give the feedback and to give an associate a second chance.

Leaders with this style tend to be more formal in the way they conduct meetings and communicate with their teams and often they rely heavily on email. For them this makes perfect sense as the instructions are clearly written and an easy source of reference for both the leader and the team member. They are task rather than people focused so often see team meetings as a waste of time unless there is a very clear need to update everyone or to solve a problem. What can then happen over time is that the team only gets together when there is a problem – so without care this can come across as a rather negative experience.

Like all the styles, they are critical for the success of a law firm. Risk-Averse leaders are the guardians of quality and they challenge other partners to keep standards high, to be compliant with regulations and to protect the firm from decisions that are too risky. They don't usually strive for leadership roles beyond partnership, but often they rise to the position of group leader or a role on the board because they are the most expert in their practice and once there, they take the role very seriously. They are quiet leaders but can be highly effective in law firms because of their need to plan and minimize risk. I have yet to meet a partner in charge of risk or compliance who doesn't have this as a leading preference in their style.

In our **ABCDE** of leadership, Risk-Averse leaders focus on **D** – ***Difficulties*** to be avoided. Their challenge is to communicate more, and more enthusiastically – highlighting and selling the vision (what needs to be ***Achieved*** and the ***Benefits***) and ensuring all plans are expressed positively (***Clarify how***).

## Does this sound like you?

1. Are you a natural perfectionist and hate to get anything wrong?
2. Is your focus on detail one of your best assets?
3. Do you rely on facts and objective arguments to persuade?
4. Do you have a very logical approach to problem solving?
5. Do you prefer logical tasks to those related to solving people problems?
6. Do you get frustrated if people haven't been clear or have withheld information, resulting in you doing a less than perfect job?
7. When communicating with others do you prefer to put it in writing/email or at least plan carefully what you are going to say?
8. Are you a bit of a pessimist and look out for problems to solve?
9. Are you quite formal in relations with colleagues?
10. Do you expect people to respect you for your expertise?

If you have got to this stage and you still don't identify more strongly with any of the four styles described, then it is likely you have a hybrid style made up of two or three preferences. The Risk-Averse style, because widespread among lawyers, is in four of the hybrid styles in Chapter 11.

# Chapter 10

# Identifying your own leadership style

In my experience, it is more common for lawyers to have a hybrid style than a single, strong preference. However, I also find that many lawyers will point to others and say 'Oh, he or she is such a …' and they identify one style. When we look at others, we often simplify things to the strongest characteristics. When we look at ourselves, we are often more aware of complexity.

Before moving onto the hybrid styles, let's look at two summaries to help you identify your preferences, even if they do tend to simplify things.

## Behavioural continuums

If you are the type of person who likes a diagram, the following might help you think about the four main styles against two sets of continuums that affect behavioural preferences.

Where are you on each of these?

During the course of a day, different situations may force you to move along any of these continuums, but you are likely to have an underlying preference. It might be at either end of the continuum or somewhere nearer the middle. The further towards one end, the more likely it is to give you a strong behavioural preference. On the following page, mark on each continuum where you think you stand.

Think carefully about the first two. All lawyers see themselves as task focused and logical because of the nature of their work. Think about them in relation to leadership activities. Do you see the team or the project first? Do you see the individual struggling or the looming deadline first?

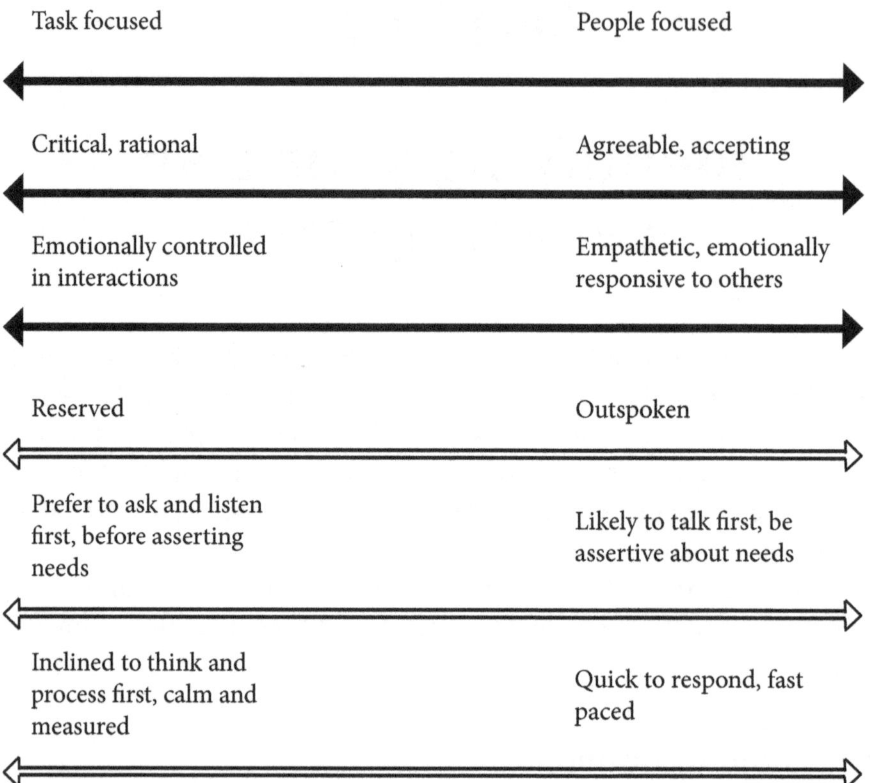


These continuums can then be mapped to create four quadrants. The first set with the black arrows run vertically, the second set with the clear arrows run horizontally. Transfer your preferences from the arrows above to the four quadrant model on page 79. You may not fall squarely into one of the quadrants but you may start to see how the behavioural preferences result in the different styles and which one/s you tend towards. If you fall mainly into two quadrants you might identify with some of the hybrid styles described in the next chapter.

On page 80 is a summary of the questions used in the chapters describing the four main leadership styles. This will make it easier for you to compare and contrast the styles. If you are still unsure, highlight the phrases that ring most true to you, in most situations at work. Although this won't capture the unique complexity of you, the column with the most highlighted phrases should identify your leading style, which may well be what others see most often. Columns with a few of the phrases highlighted are likely to be your back-up styles. Consider how often others will see this and how often you rely on these back-up styles at work. If you are evenly spread across two or three of the styles you might recognize yourself amongst the hybrid styles common in law firms explained in the next chapter.

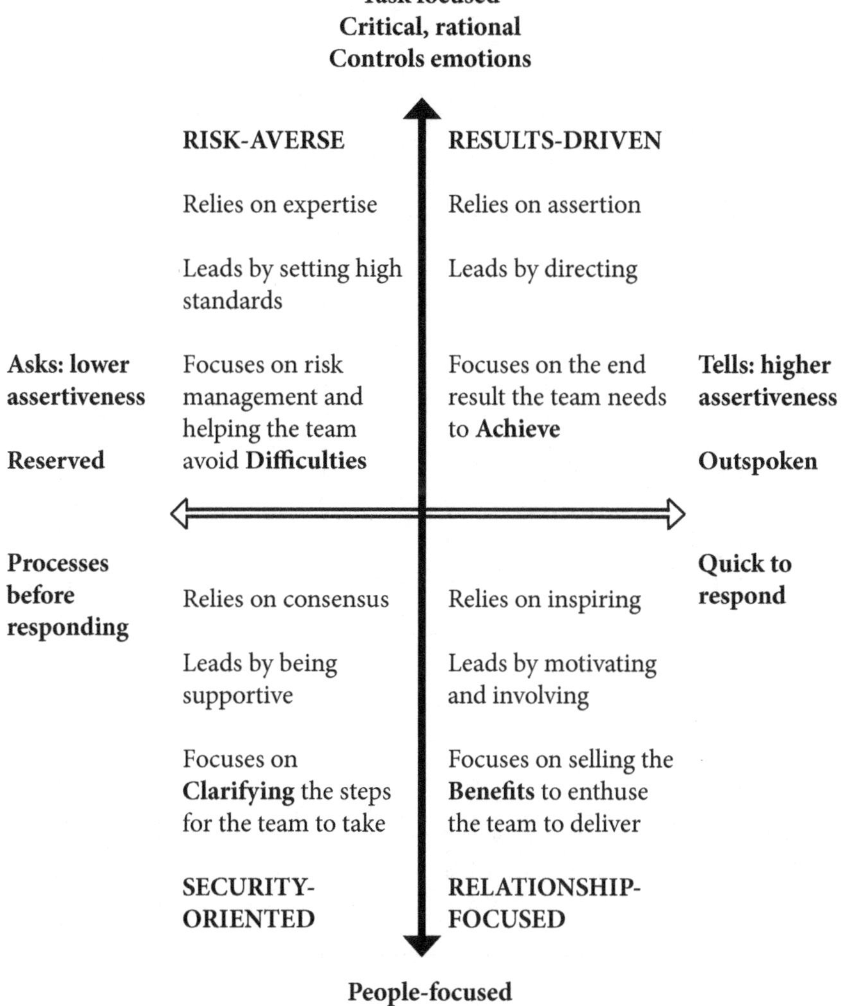

## Questions to help you identify your preferred style/s

Highlight the statements that ring true to you – at work, most of the time.

| Results-Driven | Relationship-Focused | Security-Oriented | Risk-Averse |
|---|---|---|---|
| 1. Are you driven and goal oriented? | 1. Do you prioritize relationships over results? | 1. Are you consistent and persistent, working on things until they are finished? | 1. Are you a natural perfectionist, hate getting things wrong? |
| 2. Do you have a high need to achieve? | 2. Do you have a high need to be liked? | 2. Do you prefer to listen first before providing your input? | 2. Is your focus on detail one of your best assets? |
| 3. Are you more focused on results than people? | 3. Do you like to win people round? | 3. Are you patient and appear calm to others? | 3. Do you rely on facts and objective arguments to persuade? |
| 4. Do you like to have power and exert control? | 4. Do you like to talk at length and persuade? | 4. Do you like harmony and stability? | 4. Do you have a very logical approach to problem solving? |
| 5. Are you direct and assertive in your communications? | 5. Do you like to do business in a friendly way? | 5. Do you see yourself as practical? | 5. Do you prefer logical tasks to solving people problems? |
| 6. Do you initiate? Are you a self-starter? | 6. Are you positive and enthusiastic? | 6. Do you like to focus on how things work and how things need to be done? | 6. Do you get frustrated if people haven't been clear or withheld information, resulting in you doing a less than perfect job? |
| 7. Can you be impatient and demanding? | 7. Are you optimistic? | 7. Do you like to have routines at work? | 7. Do prefer to put things in writing/email or at least plan carefully what you will say? |
| 8. Are you forceful and competitive? | 8. Are you sometimes concerned you are too trusting? | 8. Do you have set ways of doing things? | 8. Are you a bit of a pessimist and look out for problems to solve? |
| 9. Are you unafraid of conflict? | 9. Do you postpone difficult conversations, hoping things will improve? | 9. Is one of your favourite sayings: 'If it's not broken, don't try to fix it?' | 9. Are you quite formal in relations with colleagues? |
| 10. Do you relish a good argument to get to a better solution? | 10. Do you over-use praise? | 10. Are you at your most confident in familiar situations or with those you already know? | 10. Do you expect people to respect you for your expertise? |

Now that you have a framework for the four main preferences and have tried to identify your own style/s, let's look at what happens when they are blended together in hybrid styles.

# Chapter 11

# Hybrid leadership styles

## Results + Relationship: The Friendly, Fix-it-Fast leader

### Meet Charlie

Charlie is a formidable business developer and the highest billing partner in a small firm. They are young, dynamic, commercial and focused on churning through work to get quick results. Clients love the lively personality and can-do attitude coupled with the ability to cut through to the heart of a problem.

Charlie tries to inspire the team to do great things, talking of how exciting it is to do business development and encouraging them to do the same. However, most of these messages don't result in action – which is frustrating. The willing team work hard to complete the work Charlie brings in and to keep the clients happy, although work is rarely completed quite as fast as anticipated. Charlie is keen to develop the team but is often disappointed when team members don't grasp opportunities enthusiastically.

I met Charlie because things weren't going well – the firm was going through a difficult patch and desperately needed to bring in more work. Charlie had lots of ideas about what needed to change, told the partners how to bring in more business and spoke enthusiastically in partnership meetings. However, conversations with peers ended in frustration – the other partners did not follow Charlie's advice, nor did they appear to take responsibility for the situation. Several initiatives fell by the wayside when the other partners did not participate.

All this left Charlie feeling under huge pressure to bring in sufficient work to carry the whole practice and even the firm, resulting in stress, exhaustion and insufficient time to manage or develop their own team. Despite many talents and a successful career, Charlie had become the victim of trying to fix everything, leaving others passive and resentful of the constant demands to change.

The overall solution was for Charlie to slow down. Instead of rushing around telling everyone what to do, they needed to adopt a more consultative style of leadership. They had to stop saying 'If I were in your shoes, I'd …' and start asking questions to help partners solve their own issues in the way that would be best for them. This approach also worked with the team who became less passive and reliant on Charlie.

**Friendly, Fix-it-Fast leaders need to:**

- Slow it down – they tend to be fast paced and impatient
- Make the most of those relationships by asking more questions, coaching and consulting
- Ask questions to help others create their own implementation plans (**C, D** and **E**)
- Drill down, agree the specifics of the action you want and when (**C**)
- Take the time to monitor progress and help others to improve outcomes rather than keep inventing something new (**E**).

## Relationship + Security: The Country Club leader

### Meet Farah

Farah has been a group leader for many years and has built a highly successful practice with four loyal partners. Due to personal circumstances Farah is having a difficult time and has been absent from the team for four months. Without their leader, the team has faltered. Farah is the one who has all the connections and brings in the work that is then delegated not just to the associates but also to two of the partners. The partners have kept the clients happy but very little business development has been happening without Farah's galvanizing enthusiasm.

The management board asks Farah to tackle the partners who are perceived to be under-performing. Farah is accused of being too loyal to the team and too reluctant over the years to confront partners not bringing in sufficient business. They will now have to lose some team members. Redundancy will include their senior associate who was on track for partnership but is seen outside the team as a very expensive aide with no pipeline of their own.

This has left Farah demoralized and furious. The team has been a major contributor to the firm's profits for years and one small dip is suddenly an excuse to look at slimming the team down. The initial response is to go into over-drive on business development and to hand a couple of new clients over to the under-performing partners, telling them that they can develop these clients further. Farah wants them to get all the credit for this new work but is disappointed when neither partner rises to the challenge and no further instructions follow. It is at this point we meet.

It was clear that Farah was just too nice and indeed too loyal, putting up with lack lustre performance. They needed to learn how to tackle problems head-on and be clearer about what was expected rather than protecting the team. They also needed to be more articulate about the team's direction so that senior associates could create their own business case for partnership in-line with this.

The solution was to use coaching skills when managing and leading others. This suited Farah's people-oriented style but introduced more challenge and more clarity. Farah started to agree stretching performance goals and then coach in regular check-ins to ensure team members stayed focused on delivery.

**Country Club leaders need to:**

- Balance their attention on people with a focus on results/what needs to be achieved (**A**)
- Make their expectations clear upfront (**A**)
- Anticipate problems and give prompt feedback while problems are still small (**D**)
- Evaluate progress and outcomes (**E**)
- Avoid protecting under-performers
- Use their people skills to coach team members for high performance.

## Relationship + Security + Risk-Averse: The Service leader

### Meet Nuru

Nuru is one of the most popular partners in the firm. They take an interest in associates, encourage them, keep them informed, are known to be reasonable and fair. The team has good working practices and an outstanding client service ethic.

Nuru has a portfolio of very loyal clients – they are well looked after, and fee structures are kept attractive so that repeat business is guaranteed. These clients provide a broad range of work. Nuru likes the variety and is undecided about how to develop the practice over the next five years. The division head wants them to focus on the firm's top clients who are more profitable, but they prefer smaller clients where it is easier to be the single trusted advisor.

Nuru has two senior associates, both excellent lawyers who are at the stage where they should be making partner, and helps each to develop a niche. Nuru wants them brought into the partnership next year, but the division head has made it clear that the team's numbers are not good enough and the business case for each just isn't ready. Nuru is told that they need more than a niche – they need evidence of a pipeline of work and much better billing figures.

However, Nuru doesn't want to unsettle the associates who are so crucial to the team. In the annual reviews, Nuru evades direct questions about partnership prospects, instead making encouraging noises about their expertise, their value to the team and the need to continue working hard in the year ahead, particularly to increase their hours billed.

Nuru feels betrayed when first one, then the second senior associate resigns. Exit interviews reveal they both took offers of jobs with better partnership prospects and in teams with clearer strategic direction. I help Nuru plan how to make the practice more profitable, including being more confident on fees. We also develop a five-year business plan which will provide better prospects for the next associates coming through. Business development objectives linked to the firm's key clients are agreed for each team member.

**Service leaders need to:**

- Keep in sight what needs to be achieved in the longer term (**A**)
- Develop routines to step back and focus on strategy and end results (**A** and **E**)
- Set challenging goals for themselves and team members (**A**)
- Articulate expectations about performance upfront to make it easier to avoid and confront problems (**A** and **C**)
- Reframe difficult conversations as an opportunity to build stronger relationships based on honesty and trust
- Plan how to be direct and assertive with team members and clients.

## Relationship + Risk-Averse: The Charming Controller

### Meet Kai

HR ask me to help Kai since some upward feedback has revealed that they are demanding, overbearing, opinionated, a micro-manager, can easily snap, stressful to work with and one associate has lodged a grievance for bullying. Kai has been at the firm for two years and is finding it increasingly difficult to staff deals.

When busy, which is most of the time, Kai rushes around enthusiastically giving detailed instructions. They say everything is urgent and double check on progress. They have long calls or meetings to discuss what others perceive to be minor points. They are perceived to have poor organizational skills and make this worse by committing to unreasonable deadlines to super-please clients. However, once a deal completes, Kai is all smiles, thanks everyone for their super-human efforts and is highly charming.

At our first meeting I find Kai socially charming and enthusiastic. They say all the right things about the importance of motivating and developing associates and of building a team. They are interested in people and have read lots of management books. They like to share this wisdom with members of the team.

However, Kai lacks self-awareness and is not applying good management in practice, especially under pressure. They are surprised by the upward feedback and are defensive. At Kai's previous firm, it was common to engage in robust discussion about issues; challenging others was the norm and standards were very high. They think it is the best way to learn but in this firm it is seen as bullying. Although they like the associates in the team, they complain about the lack of intellectual rigour and reluctance to put in the hard work necessary to become a good lawyer.

Everything Kai says demonstrates a tension – wanting to be likeable, to enthuse others, have good working relationships with clients and teams yet being impatient, judgemental and controlling. It was hard work getting Kai to first buy-in to the need to change and secondly to adjust their behaviours. They needed to slow down and plan more. This helped them to manage client expectations and to give clearer instructions. This in turn resulted in better work product which enabled Kai to relax and develop more trust in the team to deliver what was required on time.

**Charming Controller leaders need to:**

- Keep in mind the big picture so as not to get lost in the detail (**A**)
- Highlight what needs to be achieved and provide clear priorities when delegating (**A**)
- Stop over-promising and create practical plans with realistic timeframes (**C**)
- Slow down their pace when interacting with others
- Make more use of a coaching style to help others think for themselves, instead of doing their thinking for them (**C, D** and **E**).

## Security + Risk-Averse: The Comfortable-Niche leader

### Meet Alexis

Alexis is a senior partner and the leader of a specialist group. They have been with the firm since law school and have the reputation of being a thoroughly decent human being, someone to go to if you need to talk through a sensitive or technical issue.

I meet Alexis during a post-merger integration programme in which the group leaders are being encouraged to revise their group's strategic plan to realize the benefits of the merger; to engage more with their teams who have been unsettled by the merger and to reach out to clients so that they are aware of the wider range of services now available.

Alexis is rather cynical about all this and did not vote in favour of the merger. They argue there will be few benefits for their niche, so all this post-merger activity applies to other group leaders, not to them. The Managing Partner is frustrated by their lack of engagement and refusal to do any business planning.

Our initial coaching discussion reveals that Alexis has had no experience of the value of business planning. They were in the right place at the right time and did not need to make a business case for partnership. Since then, they have strengthened the practice by providing great service, keeping the team lean and writing articles. The team is very loyal and Alexis does not think they have been unsettled by the merger, sees no need for team meetings and certainly sees no need for coaching. We have no further sessions.

One year after the merger, Alexis's team are working exactly as before but by now they are seen by all the Directors of Central Services as a problem. They have not adopted new systems, they have not integrated, and have done nothing to sell their services to partners or clients that came across as part of the merger. Alexis is furious when HR say that for the next trainee rotation, the team will not be getting a trainee. No trainee wants to join the group and HR won't force anyone to have a seat there: it is too niche a practice and operating in an old-fashioned way which won't set a good example. The Managing Partner calls me: Alexis has been told that the team is now seen as an add-on and not an integral part of the firm's service offering. Alexis is now requesting coaching.

**Comfortable-Niche leaders need to:**

- Keep an eye on the wider firm and bigger picture (**A**)
- Ensure their business strategy links with what the firm is trying to achieve (**A**)
- Build bridges with other teams and make what they do relevant to the wider firm (**B**)
- Recognize that change is increasingly fast paced in law firms

- Develop routines to review progress and identify the need to update practices/innovate to achieve more (**A** and **E**).

## Results + Risk-Averse: The DIY leader

### Meet Lou

Lou is coming up for partnership but being held back because they are spread too thin and aren't perceived to be sufficiently responsive – both on client matters and business development. They are the go-to-lawyer for a niche area of finance law and recognized expert in the market. They joined the firm 18 months earlier, moving from a firm where they worked in a very small team with minimal junior support.

In the new firm, Lou is expected to pull together a team of associates to work on deals, but they are all located in different offices. The longer-term aim discussed at recruitment is for them to build regional expertise by working with and developing these associates.

Lou is busy and finds it difficult to delegate especially across offices. They prefer to continue working alone, finding it quicker and easier to do so than invest time in getting to know and work with those who could provide support. By the time Lou recognizes that to deliver on time, additional resources are required, they find that there is insufficient time to train up an associate or there is no one available. The associates, who were initially enthusiastic about developing this area of expertise, are now staffed on other projects.

When Lou does delegate, it is at a late stage, in a rush and instructions are vague and piecemeal. Consequently, the work is not done to the standard required. They improve it but don't have time to give feedback and so the associate doesn't have a chance to learn. Mistakes are repeated. It has now got to the stage where they don't trust anyone and do it all themselves.

Lou learns to turn this around by planning to rely on others right from the start. Rather than aiming to do it all alone, they must identify a team for each matter, plan how to brief them, liaise regularly via the phone as well as email to check progress and give feedback. Lou also has to re-enthuse team members for this type of work by showing what makes the work so interesting and challenging and linking it to career opportunities – the Benefits in **ABCDE**. In order to do this, they need to spend time with the associates, find out what interests them, assess their skills and level of expertise and overall start to build a working relationship – this of course means finding reasons to visit each of the offices.

**DIY leaders need to:**

- Plan how to involve and enthuse others at an early stage (**B** and **C**)
- Plan their instructions and use questions to check understanding (**C**)
- Stop relying on email; meet or pick up the phone and have a two-way conversation (**C**)
- They are task-oriented so need to make it a task to motivate, thank and praise others for good work (**B** and **E**) by putting it on their to-do list
- Invest in developing others and providing feedback.

# Summary: Part 2

## Key takeaways

- Your leadership reputation is based on how people experience you, not your intentions, however valid they may be.
- Our behavioural preferences affect what motivates us, how we communicate, how we influence others and how we lead. When we can behave in-line with our preferences it feels more comfortable and takes less energy.
- Some people have one very strong preference where they behave consistently in-line with one of four leadership styles. However, most people have two or even three preferences – a hybrid style.
- Healthy law firms have a range of leaders with different styles. Being aware of the strengths and limitations of your own style helps you to adjust and ensure you add value to your team and firm.
- Results-Driven leaders are direct, decisive, put action first, push themselves and others. They are unafraid of conflict and like to win. They can achieve great results provided they carry their team with them. They are at risk of being impatient and of burnout. In **ABCDE** they prioritize ***Achieve***.
- Relationship-Focused leaders put people first (clients and team), are positive, communicative, friendly and rely on enthusing others to deliver. They are at risk of not being sufficiently direct or demanding. In **ABCDE** they focus on selling ***Benefits***.
- Security-Oriented leaders are practical and focus on implementation. They are more reserved, consultative, like to work in harmonious teams and often command loyalty. They are at risk of getting stuck in their way of doing things, of not innovating and of appearing too laid back or nice. In **ABCDE** they focus on ***Clarify how***.

- Risk-Averse leaders are task focused and set high standards for themselves and others. They are the guardians of quality and great risk managers. They rely on facts, logic and rules to influence. When leading they may find it harder to enthuse others since they can be over cautious and formal. In **ABCDE** they focus on ***Difficulties***.
- Combining different blends of these four styles create a range of hybrid leaders each with a mix of strengths. With two or more preferences there is a greater likelihood that more of the **ABCDE** will be included in a hybrid leader's communications, but their style can still be enhanced by ensuring all five elements are covered.

## Coming up

**A**: In Part 3 you will find out how to work effectively with different personalities – whether it's a team member, boss or client.

**B**: It will enhance your working relationships, especially with people who are different from you and whom you may find frustrating or challenging.

**C**: We'll start with how to identify someone's style and then each chapter gives you tips on how to get on the same wavelength of each of the four main behavioural styles when communicating, delegating, giving feedback, influencing and even selling.

**D**: There's lots of information here, so I recommend you dip in and out of it on a need-to-know basis.

**E**: By the end of Part 3 you should know how to refine your interactions with people who are important to your success.

# Part 3

# Aligning different personalities

# Introduction

As a leader you will find some people easy to work with and others more challenging. This part aims to give you some tips on how to adapt your own style to get better results from people who may have different motivators and different preferred ways of working to you.

Healthy law firms have a range of personalities working in them, all bringing different talents and interests to the partnership, so they need leaders who can get the best out of everyone. Similarly, clients come in all shapes and sizes so you need to be able to adapt to their style. Lawyers tend to gravitate towards the clients they work with best. However, there will always be clients who are important but trickier to manage and harder to develop the deeper relationship you seek.

Some leaders tell me that there are senior people they try to avoid too. These difficult clients or bosses are a constant source of irritation because they rarely appear satisfied, they challenge advice that others would accept or they waste the leader's time requesting things which the leader thinks unnecessary. Sometimes it is possible to avoid these people, but at other times your success may depend on getting this difficult person on board. You need to adapt your behaviours to get along with them better.

## Why you need to adapt

A frequent question in my leadership workshops is: 'I can see why it's helpful to adapt my style with senior people and clients but why should I adapt my style for team members? Surely they should adapt to me when I'm in charge!'

In an ideal world we would all adapt to some extent to the needs of others to work more effectively and collaboratively. We would all try hard to see things from the other person's perspective and to understand what is going on for them in their world. However, the only behaviours you have control over are your own. Instinctively we adapt to what will impress a client or an important senior person. It is less instinctive for some of us to adapt to the needs of our team members, yet these are the very people who can make your project a success and even make or break your career.

I have coached several lawyers on the brink of partnership who have been derailed by feedback from one or two team members indicating that they are a poor people manager, despite the lawyer also having fantastic feedback from other team members. The issue is that they aren't adapting their style to the needs of team members who work in a different way to them and have different needs.

Learning to adapt your style is also critical for ensuring you make the most of all the resources available to you. Leaders often tell me there are some team members they find a dream to work with and will try to staff on most of their projects. However, there may be two or three they find challenging, usually because of a very different style, and they avoid using these people if possible. This is a pity because those team members don't get the chance to learn from that leader. It also means that when the favoured team members aren't available, the leader struggles to make the project a success. I have known leaders try to manage without the resources they need, preferring to do the work themselves or pile it all on the one or two lawyers they want to use.

## Building diverse teams

We should also remember that healthy teams, like healthy law firms, have a range of personalities. When building a team, it is a big mistake to recruit people who are all like you because you think it will make it easier to manage them. If you do this, you will amplify your strengths but also amplify your limitations. As a leader you want a diverse team so that you can match their different talents and insights to different projects and clients. It also helps to have people in your team who like to do things that you dislike. That means when you recruit, as well as considering experience level, you should consider what gaps need filling in the short and longer term. If you have too many reserved team members, you need to seek someone who is more outgoing and will prioritize engaging with clients and bringing in work. If you have a team of optimists, you will need some lawyers who are more risk-averse to stabilize them. If you have a team that likes to do things the same way all the time, you will need to find someone who likes to challenge the status quo and who will encourage the team to innovate.

## Opposite styles can be challenging

People tend to find those with the diagonally opposite style to them, on the behavioural continuums we looked at in Chapter 10, most challenging. For example, if you are Risk-Averse you might find it more challenging to work with someone who is Relationship-Focused and vice versa. It takes more energy to adapt to someone who is on the opposite end of the continuums – it's like being left-handed but having to adapt to a right-handed implement. You can do it when necessary, but it takes focus, energy and practice.

**Task-focused**
**Critical, rational**
**Controls emotions**

**RISK-AVERSE** **RESULTS-DRIVEN**

**Asks: lower assertiveness**

**Reserved**

**Processes before responding**

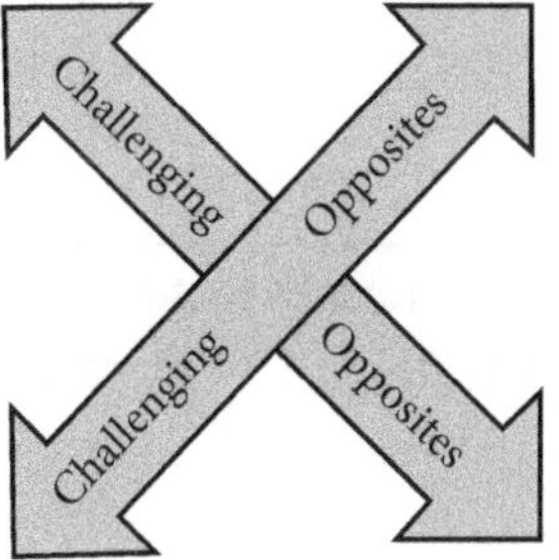


**Tells: higher assertiveness**

**Outspoken**

**Quick to respond**

**SECURITY-ORIENTED** **RELATIONSHIP-FOCUSED**

**People-focused**
**Agreeable, accepting**
**Higher emotional response to others**

We should stop seeing these people as 'difficult' and just see them as different – with different strengths and priorities. Whether a client, a boss or team member, you need to be prepared to adjust your own behaviours. It's easy to do – with small changes you can have better working relationships, be more influential and lead more effectively.

Think of one person you find particularly challenging.

| What three things do they do that you find most challenging? |
|---|
| What is the impact of this on you? If you could get on with them better, what difference would it make to life at work? |
| In what ways are they different from you or similar to you? |
| What do you think motivates them – is it the same as what motivates you? Which part of the **ABCDE** model do you think they focus on? |

## How to adapt

The **ABCDE** approach already discussed is your key tool for adapting – it helps ensure that you cover the needs of different personalities regardless of your own preferences. It forces you to focus on goals for those who are results-driven, on benefits for those who want to be enthused, on a clear action plan for those who like the security of knowing how to proceed and it ensures you have addressed potential difficulties for those who are risk-averse.

However, there are some additional behavioural tweaks you can make so that you communicate and operate on a similar wavelength.

You won't need to do this with everyone, so I recommend that you use this part of the book for ideas on how to adapt to people you find the most different or challenging, such as the person you have considered in the previous box. First, read Chapter 12 to identify the likely style of that person and then turn to the relevant chapter that deals with how to get them on board, how to align them.

There is one exception to this. Many leaders find managing those who are working from home or in another office particularly challenging. When not co-located, our different preferences seem to be exaggerated. However, even when you are on the same wavelength, it is very easy for people to feel detached and isolated from the team. Soon this can spiral into feeling no one really cares about them; work and relationships suffer. Leaders need to work much harder at communicating and engaging with their team members in these situations to avoid trust, for both parties, breaking down. In each chapter there is a section on tips for aligning team members not co-located with you and you might like to review these even for those whom you find easy to manage.

# Chapter 12

# Identifying different styles

The easiest way to identify someone's preferred style is for them to take one of the personality profiling questionnaires discussed earlier: DISC, Insights Discovery® or Social Styles. Some of the firms I work with do this – they profile whole teams and share their results openly so that everyone can adapt to each other's style. This is good practice and results in teams being more self-aware and more tolerant.

However, that's often not possible so here are some things to help you assess a person's preferred style. Think about what motivates them. In your interactions listen carefully to how they communicate, the pace of their speech, favourite words and sayings, their body language, the types of questions they ask. Then develop a hypothesis which you can check out by observing their reactions or by asking questions relevant to the way you work together such as:

- How do you want to keep in touch on this? Do you want to meet up or email?
- How much detail do you want?
- Would you like to brainstorm together, or would you prefer to have time to think this through on your own first?

You are looking for the style that you tend to see the person demonstrating most often, in most situations at work, the one that is most comfortable for them, their strongest preference. However, it's important to remember that most people are a blend of two or three styles – they may have a strongest preference backed up by another style.

The following tables list the characteristics of the four styles. As you read them you may recognize that someone has many of the characteristics belonging to one style, but also they demonstrate some elements of another style. For example, you may identify that they are strongly Results-Driven but they also share some of the behaviours of the Relationship-Focused. When you come to adapt your approach to someone's needs, you will adapt to their strongest style but also factor in adapting to their back-up styles too – so look for combinations rather than trying to restrict someone too tightly into one style.

## What motivates them?

| | |
|---|---|
| **Results-Driven** | They are very driven, competitive and self-starters. They want to win, achieve results and be in control. Sometimes a Results-Driven person will hold back because of a fear of failure, but mostly they like to be challenged. |
| **Relationship-Focused** | They are people pleasers and want positive relationships with others. Although socially confident, they like all forms of praise and recognition that they are performing well, are in the 'club', liked and appreciated. They seek to avoid rejection or the feeling of being left out. |
| **Security-Oriented** | They like to have control over their environment so prefer to have routines and know what is happening and when. They don't like surprises. This means they can feel uncomfortable if things unexpectedly change or if the goal posts move. |
| **Risk-Averse** | They are perfectionists and like to get everything right. They hate conflict, making mistakes or being in the wrong. Therefore, they like to have access to all the facts, evidence, information and rules that enable them to meet expectations and do an excellent job. |

## How do they communicate?

| | |
|---|---|
| **Results-Driven** | They are direct in their communication style, especially if this is not softened by any relationship-focus. They are assertive and tell you clearly what they think and want. They will interrupt, can sometimes be blunt and can try to take over the conversation.<br>They aren't afraid to ask challenging questions – these will relate to their aims rather than to specifics or to process. They don't mind conflict and prefer to thrash it out in a discussion. They may say things like 'Let's get to the bottom of this', 'Let's sort it out', 'Let's get this finished'. |
| **Relationship-Focused** | They are enthusiastic and friendly. They will talk at length, often referring to other people, using anecdotes and stories to illustrate their point. They will try to persuade, encourage and sell you an idea rather than tell you directly what they want. Their biggest fear is rejection, and this, coupled with their desire to please, can make them reluctant to speak directly. |

| | |
|---|---|
| | They are happy to share their thoughts and feelings with others – their communication style is relaxed and open. They tend to think it's best to meet face-to-face or to have a call, rather than relying on more impersonal forms of communication such as email. |
| **Security-Oriented** | They tend to talk in a measured way, will often be slower to respond or speak up and will usually make more tentative statements. They will question to clarify and check they have understood what is expected. They are good listeners and will listen first before talking, especially in unfamiliar situations or large meetings.<br>They are not very demonstrative and won't give away what they are thinking or feeling. It can take some time for them to trust you and until then they can be quiet and defensive. If they come across someone who is aggressive, they may take a stand on a point of principle. This can sometimes make them appear stubborn to others. |
| **Risk-Averse** | Their preference is to write rather than talk, as this means they can plan what they are going to say, get it right and include all the necessary detail.<br>They have a more formal and reserved communication style and focus on facts rather than feelings. They tend to be polite and diplomatic although they can sometimes be blunt as they prioritize accuracy over feelings.<br>They are cautious in voicing their opinion, wanting to have the perfect answer or thought. However, when they are an expert, they can be very authoritative. |

## What body language do they display?

Note this is based mainly on Western cultures.

| | |
|---|---|
| **Results-Driven** | Their body language is direct: steady eye contact, leaning forwards when interested and a tendency to point and use other hand gestures to be assertive or to take over. They may also be restless and fidgety which is linked to their impatience. This may be apparent when forced to listen to others who talk at length or at a more measured pace. They may read an email while you are talking or just look away.<br>You may also find that they squeeze a lot in and so are often running late – turning up to meetings last and leaving first.<br>When you meet them, their handshake is usually firm and can be too strong – the bone crusher. They usually offer their hand promptly and sometimes use a dominating style with their palm facing downwards to exert power over the recipient. |

| | |
|---|---|
| **Relationship-Focused** | They make steady eye contact to connect with you. They smile frequently, including with their eyes. They tend to be demonstrative, using lots of hand and body movement – even when on the phone.<br>They also may arrive late for meetings, because they were caught up in a conversation or have double-booked.<br>They have a friendly handshake and sometimes will use the double handshake to convey additional warmth. They will use touch, such as patting your arm or shoulder, as a sign of friendship or sincerity, although this is now limited in the workplace. |
| **Security-Oriented** | They appear relaxed but reserved. They will make steady eye contact while listening to you, but otherwise they are not demonstrative. They may sit back in a relaxed manner and they won't tend to use many hand gestures.<br>They will appear patient and don't like to be rushed. Because they like to focus on one thing at a time, they may forget they have a meeting and so turn up late.<br>They tend to have a straightforward, functional handshake. It is friendly, sincere and won't be aggressive or last too long. |
| **Risk-Averse** | They are also reserved and will usually look poised, with an upright posture. They aren't demonstrative, often with arms folded or holding a pen rather than using hand gestures. They usually avoid lots of eye contact, looking at or making notes instead.<br>They are punctual and so will turn up at meetings on time and get frustrated with those who run late.<br>Their handshake is usually brief and a formality. If they are not focusing on you, they might not make eye contact and might just offer the fingers. |

## Still not sure?

If you still aren't sure, here are comparisons which can help.

### Do they focus on tasks or people?

- Results-Driven and Risk-Averse people (with no relationship-focus) prioritize profits and tasks over people. They want meetings to be quick and functional with no social chit chat.
- Even in time-pressured law firms, Relationship-Focused people will make more time for supporting people, for meetings and discussion.

- Security-Oriented people like harmonious relationships so will also factor in time for people too but they will tend to do this more one-to-one.

**How much emotion do they express? Do they say 'I feel' or 'I think'?**

- The Relationship-Focused person is the most comfortable talking about their feelings and emotions. You might hear them say: 'I feel we should …'; or 'I feel it would be a good idea to …'.
- Results-Driven and Risk-Averse people will give lower priority to feelings, especially in the workplace. Results-Driven people will say 'I think …' and Risk-Averse people may talk about what they want in a more detached manner: 'We've been asked to' or 'The client wants us to'.

**How impatient? Do they have a short fuse?**

- Security-Oriented people are the most relaxed and patient.
- People with no security-orientation tend to be impatient and Results-Driven people have the shortest fuse.

**Do they like conflict?**

- Results-Driven people are the only ones who enjoy and seek out conflict, seeing it as the quickest way to get to a solution.
- Relationship-Focused people try to charm others round to their way of thinking and will be less direct in challenging.
- Security-Oriented people like an harmonious atmosphere and so prefer not to upset others, but they can take a quiet stand on something.
- Risk-Averse people dislike conflict the most as they hate being in the wrong, but if backed up by facts or rules they will challenge.

**Do they like to focus on the big picture or the detail?**

- Results-Driven and Relationship-Focused people tend to be bigger picture thinkers. They will only focus on the detail when a result or impressing a client or boss depends on it.

- Risk-Averse people focus first on the detail – they may well say: 'The devil is in the detail'.
- Security-Oriented people tend to focus on the practicalities, the details of how something will be done.

**How traditional are they versus how much do they embrace new products?**

- Security-Oriented people tend to be more conservative in their tastes and like tried and tested products, tried and tested processes.
- Results-Driven and Relationship-Focused people tend to be more open to new ways of doing things.

**How optimistic versus sceptical are they?**

- Relationship-Focused people are naturally positive and tend to be the most optimistic and can be too trusting.
- Those without any relationship-focus are more sceptical. Results-Driven people may trust their gut-feeling based on their experience, but Risk-Averse people want evidence to back-up any claim.

**To what extent do they break rules?**

- Risk-Averse people are cautious and most likely to follow the rules and the letter of the law.
- Results-Driven people will tend to bend the rules if expedient so long as the result is not jeopardized.
- Relationship-Focused people will tend to make exceptions to rules in favour of people they want to please.

# Chapter 13

# Aligning Results-Driven people

If you are Results-Driven, you are likely to find it easy to align others like you to what you want to achieve. Therefore, this chapter is for leaders who find Results-Driven people more difficult to manage or influence. It's important to remember their value to you. They expedite action and drive things forwards, focus on getting a great result for the client and making a profit. You want to harness this energy.

Overall, they are listening out for your ***Achieve*** statements. They are motivated by challenge, achieving results and by stretching goals. The following are tips to help you get on the same wavelength.

## General communications do's and don'ts

To communicate effectively it is best to:

- Let them discover things themselves
- Focus on business
- Argue facts not feelings
- Negotiate.

Avoid:

- Telling them what to do
- Giving too much detail or using too many rules
- Taking too long to do things.

To influence them:

- Focus on their goals, the big picture, the results to be achieved (**A**)
- Describe benefits in terms of profits, competing and winning (**B**)

- Provide the information they need (and no more)
- Be quick, but give them time to think
- Highlight your track record.

Words that catch their attention:

| Profit | Results | Achieve | Goal |
|---|---|---|---|
| Action | Expedite | Fast/quick | Stop |
| Drive forwards | Dive in | Initiative | Grasp opportunity |
| Compete | Win/winner | Top/first | Succeed |
| Power | Control | Take charge | Accountability |
| Ownership | Challenge | Overcome | Fail/avoid failure |
| Brief | Short | Overview | Executive summary |

## Aligning Results-Driven team members

Results-Driven team members, want a boss who:

- Gives them a challenge
- Is clear on the results needed
- Doesn't tell them what to do
- Negotiates with them.

## How would you align Katlego?

How would you motivate, delegate to and develop Katlego to achieve outstanding performance?

Katlego's team leader is finding Katlego difficult to manage. Although an excellent lawyer, efficient and noticed by clients for a responsive approach:

- Katlego ignores more routine work until it's at crisis point or Katlego dumps it on paralegals/trainees with little explanation.
- Katlego often asks for better quality work even though Katlego still has much to learn from the work allocated.
- Katlego contradicts and challenges the team leader and is defensive when given feedback.
- Some support staff have complained that Katlego is rude and over-demanding.

The following are detailed tips on delegating, developing and giving feedback to Results-Driven team members like Katlego.

## Delegating

- Always start with the aim of the matter and task – the end result that needs to be achieved (**A**)
- Give an overview of the commercial context and link this to benefits for the client (**B**)
- Give brief instructions and ask questions – they like to work it out (**C, D** and **E**)
- Give recognition to their ideas and build on them
- Be clear on what they need to check with you first and the limits of their authority: whether they can contact the client direct; whether you want them to speak up in a meeting or on a call; whether they can delegate parts of the task etc (**C**).

If they are experienced at the task, give as much freedom and responsibility as you can. This gives more challenge and they dislike being monitored so will quickly complain of being micro-managed. Get them to keep you in the loop either by copying you on emails or asking them to propose how they will update you on status and progress – agree frequency based on how involved you need to be.

When they are less experienced, you will need to manage the risk of them not being aware of what they don't know. They can easily go too far without realizing that they aren't doing the right thing. This is frustrating for them and you. Explain how your supervision will help them get a better result. For larger tasks, avoid telling them what to do by:

- Asking lots of questions when briefing such as: What issues do you anticipate? How do you think the other side will respond? How will you manage the client?
- Brainstorming ideas together
- Asking them to tell you their approach or create a plan to run by you before starting the project – guide them and fill in the gaps as needed

- Asking them to check in with you after an initial period of work on the matter or drop by their desk/call and ask them how it is going, what issues they are finding.

## Playing to their strengths and developing them

- Give them challenging work whenever you can – but tell them they will have to do their fair share of the less interesting stuff at the start of their career. For routine work, give deadlines
- Give them tasks where they can take responsibility and see an end result. They will not like being given bits and pieces
- Involve them in work for demanding clients – they will like the challenge and often impress with their can-do attitude
- Get them focused on improving the profitability of work/ providing value for money – it's usually a strength
- Help them to be more collaborative by giving them roles on bigger projects where they can't succeed alone
- Help them develop supportive relationships with others and give them feedback if they are too over-bearing or aggressive
- Stop them becoming a workaholic or being over-competitive.

## Giving feedback

It can be tricky giving them feedback as they like to challenge, even from an early stage. This means they often don't get the feedback they need.

The easiest way is to ask them to summarize what went well, what they learned and what they plan to do differently next time. This gives them the opportunity to think for themselves and you only need to confirm and add what they have omitted or where your perspective differs.

- Give praise but keep it focused on results and ideas, rather than on them
- Be direct and quick – not too much introduction or too much detail and don't rely on rules
- Focus on facts not feelings

- When things go wrong, ask questions so they see the part they played – there may be a tendency to blame others
- Where there are problems, focus on the impact, how it affects results/goals/efficiency – they may be dismissive of feedback on tasks or skills which they don't perceive to be important
- Follow-up to ensure actions are implemented.

### Aligning when they are not co-located with you

Many of the previous tips are particularly important if you have a team member working from home or in another office. Pay particular attention to:

- Checking how they most like to communicate – it may be by phone
- Being clear on how far they can go before checking in with you
- Giving clear permissions on what they can/can't do such as contacting a client
- Keeping them up-to-date on the client and bigger picture which gives meaning to their work
- Having an agreed timetable – they may rush ahead of others and get frustrated at the pace or people not responding out of hours
- Getting them to communicate with others in the team so that work doesn't fall between the gaps or they don't duplicate work
- On team video calls, asking them to put their camera on – they may think they can multi-task and not pay full attention
- Ensuring that they don't over-work; encourage them to take breaks.

## Aligning a Results-Driven boss

To get on the right side of a Results-Driven boss you need to be responsive, proactive and assertive. Many of the following tips are good for managing upwards, but particularly critical for winning the confidence and support of a Results-Driven leader.

- Be brisk and to the point, show you value their time
- Agree upfront how involved they want to be, how often they want to be updated and how they prefer you to do this. Don't be surprized if they are detached and then engage and want to change things
- Take ownership for a task – start projects promptly, update on progress and don't expect them to finish it off or fill in any gaps – work needs to be client ready
- Focus on action. Plan how you will drive a matter forwards, anticipate next steps – they like to see initiative
- Offer solutions rather than presenting a problem – they prefer to react and expect you to have done the thinking
- Be assertive when you need their attention, highlighting where their input will make a difference to the success of the matter and its profitability
- Don't hide mistakes – own up quickly and say what action you will take. Be robust in discussions but respect their experience and let them have the last word
- Focus them on what they need to review so they don't have to look at the whole document
- Be prepared to camp out in their office until they have time for you (but take work with you so you look busy and you don't waste your own time)
- For meetings offer to put together an agenda and use action verbs in the items e.g. *Agree* next steps, *Select* financing option. Use action plans to highlight who agreed to do what
- Show an interest in the profitability of matters – keep on top of the figures
- Don't expect them to take an interest in you until you have become critical to their ability to deliver great results. Don't take this lack of interest in you personally and avoid discussing personal problems.

## Aligning a Results-Driven client

Many of the tips for aligning a boss also apply to clients. In addition,

- Develop a business-like relationship, rather than a personal one. Don't be too casual or waste their time
- Show an interest in their business, the strategic aims, their goals
- Help them be seen as a winner in their organization
- Use executive summaries and headings to assist skim-reading. If they need detail, consider separating it e.g. in a text box or an appendix
- Use visuals where you can such as timelines, charts for progress, RAG (red, amber, green) tracking documents
- Offer alternatives – let them choose, make the decisions
- Focus on what you can do, not on what can't be done
- Check their preferred method of communication – they may hate emails and love texts or a quick call
- Put things in writing in case of problems – they find it difficult to admit to getting things wrong
- Show commitment to their project – make them feel as if they are your only client
- When selling to them: focus on the result they need to deliver and how you will help them achieve this; highlight where your track record is relevant; give them choices and the information they need; expect a quick decision or for it to take as much time as it takes to get to the top of their list. Close by asking – how do you want to take this forward? Be prepared to negotiate on fees or give a fee arrangement where they can say they got a good deal.

# Chapter 14

# Aligning Relationship-Focused people

This chapter is for leaders who find Relationship-Focused people more difficult to manage or influence. It's important to remember their value to you. They are enthusiastic, motivate others, build strong relationships with clients, build teams and improve morale.

Overall, they are listening out for your ***Benefits*** statements. These need to be delivered enthusiastically and to be focused on building relationships, profile, recognition and morale. The following lists give tips to help you get on the same wavelength.

## General communications do's and don'ts

To communicate effectively it is best to:

- Talk about opinions as well as ideas
- Ask how they are feeling
- Summarize in writing
- Build relationships.

Avoid:

- Arguing
- Talking facts without feelings
- Allowing them to lose respect or self-worth.

To influence them:

- Focus on client, team, relationship goals (**A**)
- Describe benefits in terms of clients, relationships, profile, morale (**B**)
- Be enthusiastic, backed by concise facts

- Highlight the impact on others
- Keep in contact but don't rush them to make decisions.

Words that catch their attention:

| Client | Relationship | Satisfaction | Empower |
|---|---|---|---|
| Opportunity | Positive | Enthusiastic | Exciting |
| Great impression | Warm | Friendly | Love/like |
| Benefit | Popular | Fan | Impressed |
| Persuade | Win round | Charm offensive | Influence |
| Talk it through | Get in touch | Reach out to | Bridge |
| Super | Great | Fantastic | Success |

## Aligning Relationship-Focused team members

Relationship-Focused team members want a boss who:

- Inspires them
- Recognizes and builds their talents, coaches them
- Makes time for them and appreciates them
- Likes meetings, believes in the value of people interacting.

## How would you align Roshan?

How would you motivate, delegate to and develop Roshan to achieve outstanding performance?

> Although Roshan is bright, enthusiastic and well connected, the team leader is frustrated by Roshan's lack of career focus and poor time management which leaves Roshan stressed much of the time:
>
> - Roshan spends too much time talking – on the phone, in meetings and when dropping by a colleague's office
> - Roshan can be impulsive and over-promises to partners and clients, resulting in long work hours for Roshan
> - Roshan gets involved in too many business development and networking initiatives, gets spread too thin and does not have time for follow-up
> - Roshan needs to be more career-focused, do more business planning, rather than trying to please everyone.

In the following are some detailed tips on delegating, developing and giving feedback to Relationship-Focused team members like Roshan.

## Delegating

- Start with the client and why what needs to be done is so important for the client (**A**)
- Highlight opportunities to interact with the client or other teams/colleagues (**B**)
- Give them the opportunity to talk about their ideas: ask questions, brainstorm (**C, D** and **E**)
- They may want to super-please and be reluctant to say 'no' so check whether they can really deliver
- Agree timelines/action plans – for larger tasks and projects, ask them to write it up
- If they don't like detail and it's important, link its importance to the impact on the client/team and how they will be perceived
- Be accessible to discuss progress.

If they are experienced, make them feel empowered to get on with the task without you and give as much access to the client or colleagues as appropriate. Agree how you want them to update you on progress.

If less experienced, they will be enthusiastic about learning and will value your time as a 'teacher'. Make time for an upfront discussion and brainstorm, show appreciation for any good ideas, but you may need to curb their enthusiasm for coming back to discuss issues too quickly before they have thought it through. They may underestimate difficulties and overestimate their ability to get things done, so agree interim checks and how you will keep in touch to check progress and answer questions.

## Playing to their strengths and developing them

- Give opportunities to interact with clients and get involved in business development, even if, at an early stage, it is only behind the scenes
- Allocate client relationship responsibilities as soon as appropriate

- Give them ambassador roles where they can make great first impressions
- They often present well, so get them delivering training and know how as this will also make them focus on technical details
- Help them learn how to plan and to prioritize
- Help them to say 'no' by getting them to think – 'If I do this what won't I have time to do?' so they see the trade-off
- Help them be less impulsive and trusting – to probe, identify risks and alternatives
- Help them develop gravitas by knowing when to say less, when to be serious and when to control displays of emotion or humour
- Focus their networking activities and ensure they follow-up
- Help them be concise and direct, avoiding a tendency to dress things up, especially difficult messages.

## Giving feedback

They are usually open to feedback and appreciate the time taken to discuss their performance. Often attuned to how others perceive them, if something hasn't gone well, they will seek out feedback. They will want you to understand what their intentions or difficulties were and to resolve the issue. They expect the feedback to be a dialogue and for them to have plenty of time to discuss solutions. For this reason, getting them to lead the feedback is as much a good idea as it is for Results-Driven people. Start with the positive 'What did you enjoy?' or 'What were you pleased with?' before asking 'What did you find more difficult?' and 'What will you do next time?'

- Give plenty of praise, credit and appreciation – they want you to notice how well they have done
- Keep the tone positive – where something has gone wrong show it is an opportunity to improve or progress
- Where there are problems, invite their ideas
- Keep feedback descriptive and non-personal. Separate the problem from the person, so they aren't tempted to dismiss the feedback with: 'They just don't like me!'
- Use written action plans to confirm the specifics
- Agree a time to meet for a quick review of progress.

## Aligning when they are not co-located with you

Many of the tips already mentioned are particularly important if you have a team member working from home or in another office. Pay particular attention to:

- Checking how they most like to communicate – it is likely to be by phone and they will appreciate video calls from time to time
- Having regular one-to-ones – they need to know you care about them and they are likely to miss the buzz of being with the team
- Giving plenty of appreciation and praise for hard work – they like their invisible work to be appreciated
- Keeping them informed about the client and plan ahead so they can be involved in client calls when relevant
- Having written and agreed timetables with interim deadlines to keep them focused on essential work – they may accept too much and may prioritize work of those with whom they are co-located or with whom they have stronger relationships
- Let them know what else is going on in the team.

## Aligning a Relationship-Focused boss

To impress a Relationship-Focused boss you need to be enthusiastic, responsive and prepared to invest time in discussion and meetings – at their convenience. Many of the following tips are good for managing upwards, but particularly critical for winning the confidence and support of a Relationship-Focused leader.

- Start off conversations with something positive
- Ask how things are going with them or their clients
- Focus on the client and the client relationship
- Agree what roles you will each play and how you will communicate with each other and the client. This is to assess how much communication they want which is likely to vary based on how sensitive they consider the client, rather than their perception of your competence
- Offer to do the planning and put together action plans, highlighting who is doing what, by when

- If you need their input, ask 'Can I have a quick five minutes of your time for ...?'
- Help them avoid difficult discussions with clients by warning them in plenty of time if fee estimates may be breached or if there are issues or delays
- Share information you have found out about the client or their sector, ideas for building the relationship and for winning new clients
- If they don't pay sufficient attention to a client, either because they are too busy or because they dislike them, ask if they would like you to take a stronger lead to support them
- Agree agendas upfront and offer to lead sections of the call or meeting so that they don't inadvertently do all the talking
- Be enthusiastic about their ideas for business or practice development, but check whether they are just bouncing an idea around or actually want you to implement it – it's possible they will move onto another new idea before you have had time to do so
- Ask for and learn from their war stories
- They often like to mentor, so be open to this and appreciate their input
- Make it easy for them to give you constructive criticism. If they only give praise, ask 'What one thing could I do next time, to do this better?'

## Aligning a Relationship-Focused client

Many of the tips for aligning a boss can be adapted for clients too. In addition:

- Invest time in building the relationship, show you are interested in them as a person as well as in their business, show you value the relationship
- Don't be too formal and be flexible: follow their train of thought, priorities and adapt to changes they want to make
- Make them look good in their organization, let them hog the limelight and be centre stage
- Be enthusiastic and positive, present problems as opportunities

- Keep things pacey but allow time for longer calls and meetings. At the start check how long they have – often optimistic, they will have booked things back-to-back and allowed less time than you may have suggested or is needed. Remind them when time is running out: they appreciate this and will often rearrange the next meeting or call if there are still important things to cover
- Address issues promptly, respond quickly before they move on to the next thing or let them know you'll get back to them soon if you need more time
- Don't get bogged down in detail or too much analysis, watch for when they are getting bored and move things on
- Offer networking opportunities and events which build links between your and their team; celebrate end of deals and projects so you can show appreciation and enthusiasm for working with them again
- When selling to them: build the relationship first; use enthusiasm backed by facts; show the impact on others – who will like it, who will be winners, how to bring any losers around. Close by saying how much you appreciated their time and how enthusiastic you are about the opportunity to work together. Ask 'What would stop us working together on your next project?' Afterwards, keep in contact but don't rush them.

# Chapter 15

# Aligning Security-Oriented people

This chapter is for leaders who find Security-Oriented people more difficult to manage or influence. It's important to remember their value to you. They are reliable, dependable, a safe pair of hands; they work in a thorough way to get things finished. They are consistent and develop specialist skills and expertise. They stabilize over-excited people and ensure things will work in practice.

Overall, they are listening out for your ***Clarify how*** plan. These need to be delivered in a measured way, step-by-step. They are motivated by being sure of how to proceed, by feeling in control of what is going to happen. The following are tips to help you get on the same wavelength.

## General communications do's and don'ts

To communicate effectively it is best to:

- Use a steady pace
- Provide information and then ask questions
- Listen patiently
- Be interested in them
- Support their ideas
- Offer guarantees.

Avoid:

- Introducing rapid change
- Changing routine or the environment
- Rushing them.

To influence them:

- Focus on goals to secure clients, enhance service and reduce disruption (**A**)
- Describe benefits in terms of securing workflow, avoiding surprises, improving brand, enabling the team to work efficiently and harmoniously (**B**)
- Focus on solutions, service standards and what will happen in practice
- Highlight successes, case studies, testimonials
- Use brand as reassurance.

Words that catch their attention:

| | | | |
|---|---|---|---|
| Client care | Satisfaction | Collaborate | Consult/listen |
| Confirm | Consistent | Practical | Reliable |
| System/systematic | Steps | Checklist | Routine |
| Experience | Specialist/skilled | Solution | Efficient |
| Finish | Complete | Reassure | Comfortable |
| Safe | Tried and tested | Guarantee | Brand |
| Best practice | Personal best | Progress | Evolve over time |

## Aligning Security-Oriented team members

Security-Oriented team members want a boss who is:

- Organized and structured
- Sets reasonable deadlines
- Develops them step-by-step
- Listens and helps them develop their ideas/get started.

## How would you align Kim?

How would you motivate, delegate to and develop Kim to achieve outstanding performance?

> Kim joined the firm one year ago, with expertise much needed in the team. Strategically, Kim is an important part of the team's wider offer. The aim is for Kim to make partner within one-two years. Kim's team leader, a very busy and driven partner, asked for Kim to have coaching: Kim just isn't matching up to expectations. Kim is:
>
> - Not billing enough
> - Not getting on with business development activities and not contacting previous clients
> - Not known outside the team, has not done enough to connect with other teams
> - Perceived to lack any sense of urgency and is leaving the office earlier than others.

The following lists are some detailed tips on delegating, developing and giving feedback to Security-Oriented team members like Kim.

## Delegating

- Where possible give one matter or project at a time; avoid dumping many things in one go
- When discussing what needs to be achieved, show where their contribution fits in and why their help is needed (**A**)
- Highlight how the work will help the team, help to secure future work or the client (**B**)
- Make time for discussing how the work will be done (**C, D** and **E**)
- If in a rush, provide the context and then agree to meet soon to confirm how the work should be done
- Break things down into distinct steps or stages
- Suggest examples of the type of thing you want
- Use checklists and action plans
- Discuss timelines and where possible ask them to propose interim deadlines so they feel in control of when they will need to deliver
- If it looks like things will take too long, ask them where corners could be cut
- For non-urgent things, agree an early time for reviewing progress of the first step to ensure that things get started

- Make it clear if you are expecting them to delegate some elements of the work, ask them who could help
- Chase late work.

If they are experienced, show you trust them and give them responsibility for the task, but make time to confirm their plans. Agree how you will review progress and fees so that things stay on track and within budget.

If less experienced, highlight the opportunity to develop their specialist skills and knowledge and say that you appreciate they will need guidance. This doesn't mean you have to provide instructions for every step of the way, but make time to sit down, ask for their ideas on how to proceed so that they don't become too passive and rely too heavily on you.

## Playing to their strengths and developing them

- Give them work that requires patience, persistence, follow-up
- They are at their best in familiar situations, so involve them in clients who give repeat work
- Ask for their ideas on how to build the client relationship
- Help them develop specialist skills and expertise valued by others – this could be technical, client or sector related
- Make introductions for them – once connected they will start to build strong and trusting relationships
- Get them into the habit of end of matter reviews to identify opportunities to improve working practices and increase efficiency
- Make sure they are using to-do lists and prioritizing, so they work at an optimum pace – very often they keep it all in their head until things get stressful and they step up a gear
- Watch out for signs of stress as they are not demonstrative and may ask for help too late
- Encourage them to speak up in meetings, ask for their ideas – they have them but are happy to let others do most of the talking
- Never set an objective without discussing an action plan to achieve it.

## Giving feedback

Take care when giving feedback as Security-Oriented team members can be more sensitive than they appear and will get defensive if they think feedback is unfair or they haven't had an opportunity to explain their perspective. Feedback can be challenging if you are asking them to make big changes to the way they do things. In this case don't rush it, make it feel collaborative, sit down together to work out practical ways forward.

- Reassure and build confidence by showing them what they have learned, how far they have come, the progress made
- Use plenty of praise but be specific or they may think it is insincere
- Show appreciation for the contribution they have made, the effort taken
- Encourage them to step up a level by saying: 'You are now ready for …, and what I'd like to see you doing next time is ….'
- When things go wrong, be clear about the impact it has had so they see the need to change
- Seek their views on the causes of problems as well as on solutions
- If you are having to impose changes, be clear about what you want and why and then discuss how to achieve this – be specific about solutions
- Follow-up to praise progress and to signal you are monitoring what was agreed (they might hope you'll forget).

## Aligning when they are not co-located with you

Many of the previous tips are particularly important if you have a team member working from home or in another office. Pay particular attention to:

- Checking how they most like to communicate – it may well be by email so there are fewer interruptions
- Having an agreed approach for raising questions – they may be less likely to want to interrupt you and wait too long before seeking clarification

- Being very clear on roles and responsibilities – who is doing what and by when
- A clear timetable with interim deadlines and a method for ensuring that they have started the work. They may be inclined to prioritize work of others who are in closer proximity. Chase late work
- Showing plenty of appreciation for work done – they will not bring themselves to your attention but may easily feel exploited when working remotely
- Checking their workload – they may not tell you soon enough when they have too much or too little
- As far as possible using the same processes, checklists, systems that they are used to using.

## Aligning a Security-Oriented boss

To win the trust of a Security-Oriented boss, you need to be reliable, measured and consultative in your approach. Avoid anything that might come across as aggressive or confrontational. Use your initiative, make suggestions but don't go too far without involving them unless they have already given you the go ahead and indicated they don't want to be involved.

- Make time for building the relationship – they like to work with people they know and trust
- Find out what is important to them, how they want to build the practice or client relationships and where you can support them
- Focus on client service
- Don't appear to compete with them – propose ideas which will showcase you as a team
- Help them focus on strategy, ask questions about direction, what needs to be achieved or how this links with what is being proposed
- Keep them informed of what is going on – they don't like surprises
- Work with their processes, routines and checklists, but suggest tweaks where you spot opportunities to update or improve them

- When proposing ideas, show you have thought things through and have got the practicalities sorted
- Introduce suggestions for change as building on what has already been done or as incremental improvements
- Avoid interrupting, agree regular catch-ups
- They can be great mentors and teachers, so consult them, ask for feedback and appreciate their insights.

## Aligning a Security-Oriented client

Many of the tips for aligning a boss can be adapted for clients too. In addition:

- Spend time getting to know them personally, identify common interests – both will help to build trust
- Get to know their business, be commercial and practical
- Show what you can do to reduce their workload
- Show you want to invest in developing good ways of working together. Joint end of matter reviews and lessons learned are highly appreciated
- Praise their team when they have been good to work with, give credit to their input
- Use timelines to reassure that, given your experience, this is how you expect the work to progress. Highlight where their input will be needed so they are not surprized when you need a document turned around quickly or a timely decision
- At the outset agree a structure and routine for reviewing progress and fees, and check that it is working for them
- If a project is long lasting, keep them focused on what needs to be achieved and review at key stages whether this has changed or needs updating
- Don't rush meetings and calls – propose a decision but give them plenty of time to feel consulted on whether they can support it, on how to make it work in practice, as well as dealing with any impact on their people
- If giving advice that their business won't like, offer to present it for them, aim to reduce internal conflict

- If they are involved in litigation, recognize the need to give comfort where you can – what may be everyday business to you, might be new and overwhelming for them
- When selling they are likely to be initially cautious, possibly suspicious, so reassure: focus on solutions, service and what will happen in practice; highlight your successes and your brand; provide case studies and testimonials so they feel comforted by who else is using you. Link fees to service levels. Close by saying how much you would like to work with them and their team and ask 'What are the next steps for you?'

# Chapter 16

# Aligning Risk-Averse people

This chapter is for leaders who find Risk-Averse people more difficult to manage or influence. It's important to remember their value to you. They are logical, concentrate on detail, follow directions, have high standards and are the guardians of quality. They are good risk managers and ensure compliance too. All of these traits are critical in law firms.

Overall, they are listening out for your ***Difficulties*** statements. These need to be delivered in a factual, analytical way showing that you have thought things through and know how to manage the risks. They are motivated by being clear about your expectations, having all the information they need and being aware of the rules so that they can do an expert and error free job. The following are tips to help you get on the same wavelength.

## General communications do's and don'ts

To communicate effectively it is best to:

- Be organized and prepared
- Give alternatives, list advantages and disadvantages
- Give things in writing
- Provide proof.

Avoid:

- Being too general
- Leaving out details
- Rushing decisions
- Making sudden changes.

To influence them:

- Focus on goals to achieve excellence and exceed client expectations (**A**)
- Describe benefits in terms of reducing risk, improving quality, developing expertise and provide evidence that these can be attained (**B**)
- Highlight what reduces risk
- Provide facts and evidence
- Encourage discussion of their concerns
- Allow time for their decision making.

Words that catch their attention:

| Think | Analysis | Objective | Advantages/disadvantages |
|---|---|---|---|
| Prepared | Plan | Problem solve | Perfect |
| Prevent | Avoid conflict | Risk management | Caution |
| Standard | Rules/policy | Review/check | Quality/quality control |
| Expert | Thought leader | Knowledge | Facts |
| Detail/in depth | Evidence | Proof | Data |
| Agenda | Report | Spreadsheet | Research |

## Aligning Risk-Averse team members

Risk-Averse team members want a boss who:

- Gives clear instructions and background information – all the facts
- Makes expectations clear, including how much authority they have
- Sets clear objectives
- Develops their expertise
- Provides work requiring high standards and precision.

## How would you align Jing?

How would you motivate, delegate to and develop Jing to achieve outstanding performance?

Jing's partner is concerned that Jing needs a more commercial approach and needs to improve the profitability of matters. Jing is not taking on board feedback to try harder at this. Jing is extremely bright, has a good legal brain and Jing's work is technically outstanding. However, Jing:

- Writes at length and in too much detail to make advice clear for the client
- Spends too long perfecting work
- Is reluctant to delegate, making some tasks expensive
- Relies too heavily on email and could often sort a problem faster if Jing just dropped by someone's desk or picked up the phone.

The following are some detailed tips on delegating, developing and giving feedback to Risk-Averse team members like Jing.

## Delegating

- To avoid them getting lost in the detail: start with the big picture and what needs to be achieved; what's important and not important to the client (**A**)
- Highlight the expertise they will develop or where their expertise is needed (**B**)
- Make your expectations very clear – deadlines, end product, level of quality required, especially if it doesn't need to be perfect (**C, D** and **E**)
- Give permissions, for example to contact the client direct, so they are not worried whether they have the authority to do this
- Be clear what is out of scope, what the client is not willing to pay for
- Clarify roles – who is doing what and encourage them to trust others to do their part
- Confirm details in writing for larger matters, use action plans, tracking documents and checklists as they hate to make errors
- As the matter progresses, keep them informed
- Make time to discuss technical issues and always bring it back to the specifics of the client situation.

If they are experienced at the task, give them ownership and permission to progress without your involvement as appropriate. They take responsibility seriously and will progress faster if it's clear this is expected.

If inexperienced, they are likely to prefer you to explain in detail what you want them to do. However, include some questions so they think for themselves. At the end ask, 'Is there anything you would like me to clarify?'

## Playing to their strengths and developing them

- Give them analytical work, research, problem solving, risk management tasks
- Give them opportunities to develop a niche, become a go-to lawyer and eventually to become a thought leader
- Ask them to write articles and contribute to know how
- Allocate parts of calls/meetings/presentations where they can talk authoritatively about work they have done. This will build their profile
- Help them to keep the bigger picture in focus – for example, ask them how a suggestion is going to help the client achieve their aim
- Encourage them to trust others, including their managers, and to learn how to 'let go' when delegating
- Get them to use outline plans to decide what is important and what can be left out, before doing too much work
- Help them to analyse risk including the risk of not doing something or delaying until all the information is available
- Encourage them to plan how to address any conflict situation directly
- Build their confidence by giving recognition to their ideas and by getting them to review regularly how much they have learned, new expertise they have developed, how they handled things better than before, etc.

## Giving feedback

Risk-Averse team members usually have very high standards for themselves and for others and are constantly on the alert as to whether these standards have been met. They will tend to focus on what didn't go well, so help them balance this by asking questions about what did go well and to identify the progress they think they have made.

- All praise must be specific – avoid general statements such as 'That was great' as they may think it is insincere or manipulative
- Use plenty of concrete examples – of what happened or what you would like to see them doing another time
- Focus on facts and evidence, not feelings
- Help them get perspective to avoid one problem or issue overriding all that has gone well
- They don't like making errors so always give them a chance to explain their perspective on what went wrong. However, discourage lengthy written justifications
- Don't get bogged down in problems – move on to solutions and agree action plans.

## Aligning when they are not co-located with you

Many of the previous tips are particularly important if you have a team member working from home or in another office. Pay particular attention to:

- Checking how they most like to communicate – it is likely to be via email
- Agree how they should raise issues with you – they are likely to be very respectful of your time and avoid interrupting you
- Make sure you have calls every so often to stop them getting isolated
- Ask them to make time for team meetings – they may prioritize other work and so get increasingly distant
- On team video calls, asking them to put their camera on will help them to re-connect with the team
- Make sure you keep them up-to-date and give them the bigger picture – they don't like to be missing information that would help them to do a good job
- Build trust by being very clear on expectations when delegating, especially if a job needs to be done quickly rather than perfectly
- Encourage them to delegate when appropriate – it is easy for them to get into a do-it-yourself rut when working from home.

## Aligning a Risk-Averse boss

To win the trust of a Risk-Averse boss you need to be respectful, planned and be on top of the detail. Many of the tips are good for managing upwards, but particularly for gaining the confidence and respect of a Risk-Averse leader.

- Be punctual and prepared for meetings
- Focus on quality and risk – do the best job you can
- Show an interest in discussing technical issues and their analysis
- Avoid directly challenging them and back up your points with facts and evidence
- Be clear when you need their input/expertise on tricky issues – this helps them to trust your judgement and reduces any tendency to want to micro-manage
- Clarify roles upfront to avoid potential conflict or confusion and check how far they want you to go without involving them
- If you are ready for them to be more hands-off, propose what you could do and agree how you will update them
- Don't take risks or be spontaneous – be compliant with rules, policies etc.
- When giving them something to review, indicate if you are unsure about a certain issue or section so they focus on that rather than the whole thing
- Don't take their revisions to your work personally and show you have learned from their comments
- Don't rely on them to pick up on typos or small errors – they will spot them a mile off but will think you can't be trusted if you haven't produced the best work you can
- Remind them of the bigger picture and client priorities if they get lost in detail
- Be proactive in updating on progress against fees.

## Aligning a Risk-Averse client

Many of the tips for managing upwards also relate to building stronger relationships with Risk-Averse clients.

- Schedule meetings and calls and provide agendas
- Temper your enthusiasm; show an interest in the work but don't come across as too excited
- Spend time at the instructions stage, ensuring you are clear on what is in scope and out of scope and ensure this is confirmed in writing
- Allow time for detailed discussions, and don't interrupt
- Ask analytical questions to help them focus on what's most important, such as 'What are the three key things that will make this a success for you?' or 'What are your top two concerns at this stage?'
- Don't assume that silence is a sign of agreement
- Look at alternatives – the advantages and disadvantages of each, rather than brainstorming possible solutions
- Link any scope creep to additional costs and check whether this will help achieve the overall goals – is this something that is really necessary or just a nice-to-have?
- Check how much detail they want to see
- Highlight where action or decisions need to be taken – visually separating it from the detail for example, by using bold text or headings
- Provide reassurance that you are on top of the detail
- Provide legal updates, newsletters, things you think will be of particular interest to them and their business
- If advice is going to be unpalatable to their business, help them present it to reduce the need to confront problems head-on, and give them plenty of back-up evidence that this is required
- When selling: focus on how your expertise will reduce risks; provide facts and evidence; encourage discussion of their concerns; link cost to expertise, quality and risk; and allow time for making the decision. Close by confirming your interest in working with their business and asking 'What further information do you need before making a decision?'

# Summary: Part 3

## Key takeaways

- Healthy law firms have a range of personalities and you need to be able to work with and influence all of them. It is up to you to adapt since you can't control the behaviour of others.
- Getting on the same wavelength as someone who is different from you will help you support and align them so that they deliver the results you need.
- You can identify someone's style by finding out what motivates them, how they like to communicate and even the body language they display.
- The **ABCDE** tool ensures that at some point you will address what different personalities need to hear.
- Results-Driven team members want you to be direct but don't like to be told what to do. Give them a challenge and responsibility as soon as you can; help them work collaboratively.
- Results-Driven bosses and clients want you to be brisk, direct, proactive and responsive. Avoid detail and focus on the big picture and make-or-break issues.
- Relationship-Focused team members want to be inspired, appreciated and coached. Give them opportunities to interact, especially with clients; help them be more direct, avoid over-promising and to develop gravitas.
- Relationship-Focused bosses and clients want you to be enthusiastic, make time to talk and invest in the relationship. Present problems as opportunities and make them look good.
- Security-Oriented team members want you to be organized and reasonable about deadlines. Give them checklists and action plans; develop them step-by-step.
- Security-Oriented bosses and clients want you to be reliable, measured and consultative. Avoid surprises, don't rush interactions and keep things practical.

- Risk-Averse team members want you to give clear instructions and enable them to do a perfect job. Give them opportunities to develop their expertise, even a niche; help them to avoid getting lost in the detail.
- Risk-Averse bosses and clients want you to be respectful, planned and on top of the detail. Stick to the facts, temper your enthusiasm and bring their attention back to the bigger picture.

## Coming up

**A**: Parts 4 and 5 give you two toolkits for planning conversations about a project – whether internal or for clients – and for one-to-one conversations with team members about their performance.

**B**: Each tool ensures you cover the **ABCDE** for that situation – so you don't miss things; it will save you time as well as help you have more motivating and effective conversations.

**C**: Each tool is a checklist of questions or bullet points to consider. Part 4 includes tools for scoping and planning a project, for briefing the project team and delegating, for monitoring and reporting on progress and outcomes. Part 5 gives you tools for one-to-one conversations with team members – when they join your team, to adjust your supervision approach when delegating, to give feedback and develop them.

**D**: Again, there is lots of information here, so I recommend you turn to the relevant tool when you need it rather than reading them all through. A list of tools is provided at the start of Parts 4 (p. 141) and 5 (p. 169) and also on the Contents pages (pp. ix–xi).

**E**: After using these tools, you should find that you are leading more effectively and that the **ABCDE** approach starts to become second nature.

> I have already followed the **ABCDE** toolkit this morning during my discussion with my Partner and it worked!
>
> *Senior Associate, Magic Circle Firm*

# Part 4

# Tools for project conversations

# Introduction

Over the last ten years, lawyers have been under increasing pressure to deliver more for less – whether for clients or when working in-house for the business. This has shone a spotlight on working more efficiently and on project management. For some large, high risk, cross-jurisdictional projects it is now common to have a professional project manager supporting the teams of lawyers so they deliver on time and budget without work being duplicated or falling through the cracks. This is the case in-house as well as in private practice.

However, it isn't the norm for the majority of matters, deals, transactions and cases where the lawyer leading the team is expected to ensure the project is managed smoothly. Lawyers have had to develop the basic skills for project management. These tools are to help you if you have this role or if you are assisting someone responsible for managing the project such as a busy partner.

You won't need them for every project. If you are leading a matter and it is business as usual and the matter and team are small, you are unlikely to need to use all the tools or you can pare them back to the minimum. For larger projects they are checklists which distil good project management practices in an easy-to-follow manner. They get you to plan conversations with the client or team at different stages of a project so that you are always clear on what needs to be achieved, you enthuse the team and help them to deliver the project smoothly. They will help you impress your team and your client.

This toolkit uses the **ABCDE** which by now should be familiar to you. Throughout, 'project' is used as a general term to cover a matter, a deal, a transaction, a case or an internal project. If using for internal projects, where 'client' is referred to this will be the internal client or project sponsor or key stakeholders.

Each tool gets you to think about:

A — *Achieve* – what the team needs to achieve, what you want the team to deliver.

B — *Benefits* – why the project is important to them, the team, firm, client, etc.

C — *Clarify how* – the steps the team will take to deliver the project.

D — *Difficulties* – how the team should avoid or manage any difficulties and risks.

E — *Evaluate* – how you will evaluate the team's progress and project outcomes.

When using the tools, pay attention to the sections that you might usually ignore or not prioritize because of your preferred leadership style. They are likely to feel less instinctive, perhaps even frustrating – but they will make your leadership of a project more effective.

| **If you are** | **You will prioritize** | **Supplement with** |
|---|---|---|
| Results-Driven | *Achieve* | **B**enefits to motivate the team; and slow down the discussion to ensure there is an agreed plan for implementation covering **C, D** and **E** |
| Relationship-Focused | *Benefits* | **A**chieve to focus the team on the end result; and ensure you pay sufficient attention to possible **D**ifficulties when discussing **C, D** and **E** |
| Security-Oriented | *Clarify how* | **A**chieve and **B**enefits to create focus and enthuse the team; and **E** to keep things on track and create momentum |
| Risk-Averse | *Difficulties* | **A**chieve and **B**enefits to start the conversation positively and to provide the bigger picture. This will both motivate and make it easier for the team to know where to focus their efforts |

Also consider your audience – what are they wanting to hear you address? On projects, you will usually have a range of team members with different styles, who will each be listening out for the section that motivates them. If you are having a one-to-one conversation on a project, you might emphasize the section that is most relevant to that team member's preferred way of working and use the aligning tips for them in Part 3.

The toolkit includes the following tools. I hope you find them useful.

- Planning an initiative/change
- Scoping a project
- Planning a project
- Briefing the team
- Delegating part of a project
- Reviewing progress
- Reporting progress upwards/to stakeholders
- Conducting an end of project review (or end of stage)

# Planning an initiative/change

You've got a great idea! **ABCDE** can be used to help you plan an initiative or a change in your team or firm. This tool is for internal projects and comprises a checklist of questions to consider at the outset as you test the viability of your idea. It is based on overcoming common barriers to initiatives and change in law firms. If you are not the initiator, you may find the checklist on 'Scoping a project' more relevant.

| | |
|---|---|
| A | ***Achieve:* What do you want to achieve?**<br>You need a clear vision of what the initiative/change will achieve in, say, six months or a year.<br>• What will be the end results of the initiative/change? What will it achieve/improve?<br>• What will success look like?<br>• What are you expecting people to do (not do) as a result of the initiative/change?<br>• Can you create a single sentence to describe the vision? |
| B | ***Benefits:* Who will benefit and how will you get them on board?**<br>Now you need a compelling business case for this change/initiative. You also need to consider how you will inspire others to support it and back the investment of time/money.<br>• What is the business case for the initiative/change?<br>• What are the benefits for the team, your clients and the firm?<br>• What incentives are there for people/stakeholders who will need to adopt the change?<br>• How does the initiative/change link with the firm's/your strategy and values?<br>• How can you link team members' aspirations and values to the initiative/change?<br>• What are the costs versus these benefits?<br>• What is the urgency? What are the competitive drivers?<br>• What are the risks of not doing this/not changing?<br>• Why should it be prioritized over other projects or be given the same priority as fee earning?<br>• Which key stakeholders/important opinion-formers will support it?<br>• Is your 'boss' committed to the proposed initiative/change?<br>• Who will be winners and how can you get them to champion or support it?<br>• What coalitions can you build with other teams to support the initiative/change? |

<table>
<tr><td>C</td><td>Clarify: What needs to happen and how will you build momentum?<br><br>Too many great ideas never get implemented because they are floated without considering the practical implications of making them happen.<br><br>• What steps need to be taken? Do you have an action plan?<br>• How long will it take to implement? Do you need to create urgency? (If things take longer than six months in law firms, the initiative/change usually loses too much momentum and dies.)<br>• Do you have a timetable with milestones?<br>• Does it identify short-term gains (quick wins) to motivate and keep support high, this is especially important if it will take longer than six months?<br>• Will you pilot test the change first in one area and then expand to others?<br>• What longer-term action will be required, if it will take a long time to implement fully?<br>• Have you considered how the change will be embedded? For example: What working practices are in-line or need to be adapted? What regular communications/meetings and reward systems can be used to support the initiative/change?<br>• What resources will you need – people/time/budget?<br>• How will you use champions? Who will you get involved to help you with implementation? How will you get their buy-in and do you need to get the buy-in from their bosses to enable them to assist? How will you assign accountability for actions?<br>• How will you brief the team and individuals at the start? How will you keep people up-to-date and on board?<br>• For more detailed planning, you can use the Clarify how section of the ‘Planning a project’ tool.</td></tr>
<tr><td>D</td><td>Difficulties: How will you overcome resistance and difficulties?<br><br>Anticipate what could stop your great idea, what could derail the initiative/change. In law firms, resistance is most likely to be from people or because fee earning takes priority.<br><br>• Who will resist the change? Who will be the losers? For whom will it create difficulties?<br>• Who might be cynical and think the change can’t be achieved or that it is too risky?<br>• How can you reduce the impact of their resistance?<br>• How will you balance implementation with the focus on day-to-day work and fee earning?<br>• What are other possible obstacles/risks?<br>• How will you avoid raising unrealistic expectations that could later be used to question the viability of your initiative/change?<br>• What systems will need to be adjusted to be in-line with the initiative/change so that they don’t undermine your efforts?</td></tr>
</table>

| E | ***Evaluate:*** **How will you review and communicate progress and outcomes?**<br>Thinking about how you will evaluate progress and outcomes before you start will ensure that you have set realistic goals for the initiative/change. If necessary, go back and tweak your vision of what will be ***Achieved*** and the ***Benefits*** if you realize these are not realistic.<br>• How will you measure and manage progress against milestones?<br>• How long before the partners/stakeholders expect some quick wins/results?<br>• How will you use communications to both report progress and keep alive support for the initiative/change?<br>• How and to whom will you report on the outcomes of the initiative/change? |
|---|---|

# Scoping a project

ABCDE gives a framework for asking questions of your client starting with the big picture and then planning what needs to be done. It can be used for internal projects in which case the 'client' referred to in the tool will be internal clients or stakeholders.

| | |
|---|---|
| A | ***Achieve:* Identify what the project should achieve**<br>You need to develop a good understanding of what the client (or for internal projects – what the firm/project sponsor) wants to achieve so that you can identify priorities and what could be excluded from the scope of the project. Sample questions for discussion include:<br>• What do you want to achieve?<br>• What are the commercial drivers/goals?<br>• What are the three most important things you want to achieve on this project?<br>• What will be the key indicators for you that this project has been a success? |
| B | ***Benefits:* Identify the benefits for the client and their stakeholders**<br>Before getting into the detail of planning the project, check the value of the work to the client and stakeholders – it must be greater than the investment cost.<br>Assessing the benefits and value to the client will help you price the work or decide an appropriate budget for the project. Later it will help you to demonstrate the return on the time and costs invested in the project.<br>Sample questions for the discussion include:<br>• How does this fit with your strategy?<br>• How important is this project to your organization?<br>• How will your own clients/end users benefit?<br>• What is at risk if the project fails?<br>• How will the project enhance your reputation/competitive edge/market share?<br>• What savings will the project achieve: time, costs, efficiencies, reduced hassle?<br>Many of these questions are also applicable for identifying the benefits for your own team:<br>• Does this fit with our team and firm strategy?<br>• How will it enhance our reputation/track record/profitability?<br>• How will it benefit our own team? (e.g. opportunities for individuals to gain experience, raise their profile or develop new contacts) |

<table>
<tr><td>C</td><td>Clarify: Clarify what needs to be done<br><br>Now you can start to discuss how you plan to deliver the project. At this early stage you are aiming to demonstrate your experience of handling similar projects but at the same time have an open discussion with the client to get their buy-in to your approach and to hear what they want and don't want to see.<br><br>Sample questions for the discussion include:<br>• The key steps to be taken: 'How do you want to approach this?' or 'We usually proceed as follows … would that suit you?'<br>• The timetable: 'What timetable do you have in mind?' or 'We usually find a timetable such as this works ….'<br>• The team: 'I would propose using the following team ….'<br>• Communication plans: 'How do you want to be kept informed?' or 'Would you like one point of contact or several?' or 'What internal decision making procedures do we need to factor in?'<br>• Budget: 'What budget did you have in mind?' or 'Would you like us to put a proposal together?' Or 'This usually costs x and we control expenditure by doing the following ... Would that suit you?'</td></tr>
<tr><td>D</td><td>Difficulties: Anticipate what difficulties need to be avoided<br><br>If this hasn't already been covered, it is worthwhile anticipating problems and difficulties and how they can be avoided.<br><br>Identify key risks, how the client wants these managed and anything that could derail the project.<br><br>Sample questions to discuss potential difficulties include:<br>• What problems do you anticipate?<br>• What else could derail this project?<br>• We often find this is an issue and we handle it as follows …<br>• Who might have difficulties with what you are proposing to do/achieve?<br>• What else do we need to be aware of …?<br>• How do you want us to notify you of any risks we identify as the project progresses?</td></tr>
</table>

<table>
<tr><td>E</td><td>Evaluate: Agree how progress and outcomes will be evaluated<br><br>By focusing on how you will monitor progress and the success of the project, you end the conversation on a positive note.<br><br>Sample questions to discuss with the client are as follows:<br><br>• How do you want us to update you on progress? How often? In what format?<br>• What are your internal reporting procedures for this project and how can we help with that?<br>• The first stage will be ... Once this is completed would you like a review?<br>• At the end of the project, how do you want to evaluate the success of the project?<br>• You mentioned that key indicators of the success of the project for you are [...], how do you want to evaluate these at the end?</td></tr>
</table>

# Planning a project

Once you have scoped a project, you can use the **ABCDE** framework for more detailed planning. You can do this planning on your own or you might delegate it to an experienced team member or do it with the team. Project plans should be documented so they can be given to the team and relevant parts to the client (or to project sponsors if an internal project). If kept up-to-date they can be useful if new team members join at a later stage.

Planning in this way helps you to be proactive as the project progresses – you have anticipated what will happen and are more prepared to control events as they unfold.

| | |
|---|---|
| A | ***Achieve:* Document the project goals, objectives or outcomes**<br>Document the commercial context and drivers of the project and the outcomes the project needs to achieve. Here it can be useful to list key indicators of success which need to be achieved. |
| B | ***Benefits:* Document the benefits for stakeholders**<br>• Document the anticipated benefits for the client (or firm if an internal project) and the value that they represent compared to the cost of the project. This may need to include the commercial costs of the project failing.<br>• Document the benefits for other key stakeholders such as the client's own clients or end users.<br>• Document the importance of the project to your firm such as revenue, client relationship, pipeline of future work, market reputation.<br>• Document any specific benefits for your own team members e.g. learning experience, internal or external profile and contacts (so that these don't get over-looked as the project progresses). |
| C | ***Clarify:* Create detailed plans of what needs to happen**<br>Clarify in detail the steps to be taken to complete the project. Document the plans so you can share them with the team and relevant parts with the client:<br>• List the **key deliverables** and breakdown the work into activities that must be completed to create these end products.<br>• Plan the **timetable** identifying what needs to be completed and by when.<br>• If the project is large divide it into smaller stages to get more control.<br>• Work backwards from your end deadline and create interim deadlines or milestones for each stage that need to be reached if the project is to progress smoothly. |

| | |
|---|---|
| | • Then assign the activities (you have already identified) to the relevant stage of the timetable, so that completion dates are clear.<br>• If a complex project or a project with an aggressive timeline, then it can help to plot these on a graphical timeline (like a Gantt chart) so that you, your team and your client can see the flow of work.<br>• Plan **roles and responsibilities** including who will lead the project on a day-to-day basis.<br>• Plan how the team will **communicate** and update each other, how decisions will be made and issues escalated.<br>• Plan how you will update the client, other parties and key stakeholders.<br>• Plan how you will launch the project – brief the team – so that they are clear and motivated.<br>• Plan other **resources** you need to complete the project and when they will be needed.<br>• Plan **quality control procedures**: quality standards to be followed/review procedures/sign offs/pilot tests etc.<br>• Plan the **budget**: estimate the input you will require, any costs and expenses. Include third party costs where appropriate and if you are managing on behalf of the client.<br>• For a top-down budget where the price is fixed by the client or the market, with the relevant teams discuss how to apportion the budget and then identify who and how the work can be completed within budget.<br>• For a bottom-up budget: once you have identified the work that needs to be done, identify who will do it, how long it will take and create a budget for each stage of the project. Discuss estimates with relevant teams – don't assume how much time or work will be required or you won't get their buy-in to the budget or the timetable. This is especially important if you are working across jurisdictions where you may unwittingly make false assumptions about how the work will be done or how much work is involved.<br>• Plan how you will sell the budget/price to the client and demonstrate the value it will provide.<br>• Plan how you will monitor the budget, keep control of costs and update the client on fees. |
| D | ***Difficulties:*** **Anticipate difficulties and how to avoid them**<br>• Review your plans for bottlenecks and create contingency plans where you can (e.g. in your timeline and in your budget) to address any risks.<br>• Identify and list possible risks (for the firm and your team as well as for the client), the source of each risk and the likely impact of each.<br>• Then plan how to monitor and handle the risks. For some risks there is nothing you can do other than accept them, but for others consider how they can be avoided, reduced, shared or transferred to other parties and any back-up plans required. |

| E | *Evaluate:* **Plan how to monitor progress and outcomes**<br>• Document how you will monitor and report on progress and to whom e.g. daily/weekly/monthly.<br>• Plan how you will review outcomes of each stage of the project.<br>• Plan how you will measure the key indicators of success for the project which you listed in **A**.<br>• Finally document how you will escalate any decision to abandon the project if events do not go according to plan and the project is no longer commercially viable for your client. |
|---|---|

# Briefing the team

ABCDE can be used to brief the team. This is a critical meeting where you need to set direction for the team and motivate them. Sounding enthusiastic about what needs to be done helps, but you also need to put yourself in the team's shoes and address what they are likely to be thinking and what they want to know.

<table>
<tr><td>A</td><td>Achieve: On this project this is what we need to achieve…<br>At the start of a briefing meeting, the team will be thinking:<br>• What's this all about?<br>• What's the big idea?<br>You need to start by describing the aims of the project. This starts the meeting positively, sets direction and provides the big picture, the context for the project.</td></tr>
<tr><td>B</td><td>Benefits: These will be the benefits…<br>Once the team has the overall picture, they will want to know why this project is important. You need to enthuse them as they will now be thinking:<br>• Is it worthwhile?<br>• Why should I prioritize this rather than other work?<br>• What's in it for me?<br>To address these thoughts, list the benefits:<br>• For the client<br>• For the firm<br>• For your team<br>• And where you can, highlight benefits for the project team members.<br>This section is critical for providing a strong sense of purpose and aligning team members' interests with what you need to achieve.</td></tr>
<tr><td>C</td><td>Clarify: Let me clarify what I'll need from you…<br>By this stage you should have enthused your team and now they are ready to hear what you want them to do so you need to address their practical questions which are likely to be:<br>• How are we going to do this?<br>• What do you want from me? And by when?<br>• Who else is involved?<br>• How are we going to co-ordinate our work and make decisions?<br>• What support have we got?</td></tr>
</table>

| | |
|---|---|
| | • What budget have we got? What fee has been agreed?<br>• What tracking documents will we use?<br>Provide timetables, action plans, team structure chart/contacts list, budgets, template tracking documents, etc. If your team is experienced, run this part of the briefing as a discussion and agree how you want them to develop the action plan, timetable, tracking documents, etc. |
| D | ***Difficulties:*** **I'm anticipating these difficulties we'll need to overcome…**<br>At this stage the team is likely to be thinking:<br>• This all sounds very good but ...<br>• How are we going to deal with …?<br>• I'm concerned that ...<br>Here your aim is to pre-empt the difficulties that your team will face by explaining how problems can be avoided and risks managed. However, it is also a chance to ask the team to raise issues and concerns that you may not have anticipated so you can plan how to tackle these together. In this case ask:<br>• What have I forgotten?<br>• What problems do you anticipate?<br>• What could hold things up/create a fee over-run? |
| E | ***Evaluate:*** **This is how we will evaluate progress and outcomes…**<br>By the end of the meeting the team should be clear what is expected of them but some might be a little cynical that today's enthusiasm will not translate into action or they may be concerned how their performance will be assessed. In this final stage, address questions your team may have such as:<br>• Once we get started, how are we going to know if things are working?<br>• How are you going to monitor and evaluate our progress and whether at the end it is successful?<br>• How is my/our performance going to be assessed?<br>Describing how you will assess progress and outcomes reinforces your determination to make good progress and that you won't let things drift along. It also ends the meeting on a positive note focused on successful outcomes. |

# Delegating part of a project

You can use the **ABCDE** approach when delegating part of a project to a workstream or team member. Adjust your supervision approach, depending on their level of experience, confidence and motivation. For additional help with adjusting your supervision approach for individuals see the one-to-one tool on delegating in Part 5.

| | |
|---|---|
| A | ***Achieve:* This is what we need to achieve overall and what I want you to do…**<br>• Provide the context for the task or part of the project that you are delegating by giving a brief overview of the whole project.<br>• Describe what needs to achieved on this workstream or task.<br>• Explain how their part will contribute to the success of the project. |
| B | ***Benefits:* This is why your task is important and what you will get out of this…**<br>Once you have described the importance of the task for the project, focus on what the workstream/team member will get out of working on this task/part of the project.<br>This could be:<br>• New expertise<br>• An opportunity to take on more responsibility<br>• Working with an interesting team<br>• Increased profile with a client, partners or part of the firm<br>• An opportunity to work on something closely aligned to their values. |
| C | ***Clarify:* Let me clarify what I'm expecting you to do…**<br>Next discuss what needs to be done. Your approach here will depend on their level of experience, confidence and motivation.<br>You can describe what they need to do if they are very inexperienced.<br>Alternatively, use questions if you want them to be more actively engaged, especially to make use of their experience.<br>For example:<br>• How will you approach this?<br>• What are the key steps you need to take?<br>• Who will you need to consult?<br>• How much time might it take?<br>• How will you work to this timetable/meet this deadline?<br>• What resources do you need?<br>• When do you want to meet to discuss your plan of action/first draft? |

<table>
<tr><td></td><td>• How will you co-ordinate with others working on other parts of the project?<br>• How can you work within the budget/agreed fee?</td></tr>
<tr><td>D</td><td>Difficulties: Let's think about any difficulties you'll need to overcome…<br>Help the team/team member anticipate what could go wrong and discuss how to avoid problems. Again, you can use questions to get them thinking actively. Sample questions include:<br>• What problems do you anticipate?<br>• What ideas have you got for tackling these?<br>• What else?<br>• How can we minimize these risks?<br>• What support will you need?</td></tr>
<tr><td>E</td><td>Evaluate: Let's agree how we will evaluate progress and outcomes…<br>Now get them to pull it all together into a plan and then discuss and agree:<br>• How to review progress against the plan. This will depend on their level of experience and level of risk represented by their part of the project. If inexperienced or the work is high risk, you will need more interim reviews.<br>• How to update the client, team or other stakeholders on progress and outcomes of their task/part of the project.</td></tr>
</table>

# Reviewing progress

Use the **ABCDE** approach to ask questions and encourage the team or a team member to take responsibility for updating you on progress with the project or their task and then to update plans for the next stage of work. The discussion can be supported by the team/team member presenting tracking documents, RAG reports (red, amber, green) etc.

<table>
<tr><td>A</td><td>Achieve: What have you achieved since we last met?<br>This is an opportunity for the team/team member to get recognition for successes and to assess whether sufficient progress has been made towards planned milestones or deadlines.</td></tr>
<tr><td>B</td><td>Benefits: What are the main benefits of what you have done so far?<br>This is to check that the time spent was worthwhile and in-line with the objectives and benefits for the client or stakeholders.<br>It will also help to keep the team/team member focused on the commercial priorities of the project and not get side-tracked by additional but lower priority tasks.</td></tr>
<tr><td>C</td><td>Clarify: What are your next steps?<br>The aim is to update the plan for the next stage of work and identify where the team leader's input is required:<br>• Key activities<br>• Timing<br>• Resourcing<br>• Cost implications.</td></tr>
<tr><td>D</td><td>Difficulties: What difficulties do you anticipate?<br>The aim is to anticipate any new difficulties for the next stage of work and again identify where the team leader's help may be required or where client or stakeholder expectations may need to be managed.</td></tr>
<tr><td>E</td><td>Evaluate: When do we next need to evaluate progress?<br>Agree when you next need to meet to evaluate progress. Frequency of progress reviews will depend on the level of activity and how much support the team/team member needs.</td></tr>
</table>

# Reporting progress upwards/to stakeholders

Use the **ABCDE** approach to update your client, the partner in charge or other key groups of stakeholders on progress with a project. Use tracking documents to support your report.

| | |
|---|---|
| A | ***Achieve:* This is what we have achieved on the project since we last met...**<br>Don't give an account of what you have done. Summarize key achievements, results and progress on the project – the focus is on the overall picture not details.<br>Often it is useful to update on the time spent and any costs in relation to progress towards outcomes. For example: we are 50% of the way through the project but we have spent 55% of the budget. |
| B | ***Benefits:* The main benefits of this work so far are...**<br>Show the value of the work completed so far by summarizing any benefits already achieved – focusing on those most relevant to the stakeholder group you are addressing.<br>Some benefits won't yet be delivered, but you might already have:<br>• Saved time/costs/reduced hassle<br>• Created a better position/terms/better opportunities<br>• Achieved some of the commercial aims<br>• Reduced or transferred risks<br>• Made improvements<br>• Started to see a return on investment<br>• Protected reputation or relationships. |
| C | ***Clarify:* These are our next steps...**<br>Outline your plans for the next stage of work focusing on any changes. Only provide as much detail as required by the client or the stakeholder group. Draw their attention to any input you will need from them.<br>Outline:<br>• Key activities<br>• Timing<br>• Resourcing<br>• Cost control. |

<table>
<tr><td>D</td><td>Difficulties: You need to be aware we are addressing the following…<br>Summarize anticipated difficulties and how you plan to deal with them. This needs to come across as proactive rather than a series of complaints! You are aiming to manage client and stakeholder expectations; to highlight where you may need to make difficult decisions; to identify where you may need input or support from the client, partner in charge or other parties.<br>Consider:<br>• Issues/changes to the scope of the project<br>• Difficulties created by the other side/other parties<br>• How you will be addressing risks in the next stage<br>• Anticipated timing or budget changes.</td></tr>
<tr><td>E</td><td>Evaluate: When would you like to meet again to evaluate progress?<br>Agree when and how you will evaluate progress in the next meeting.</td></tr>
</table>

# Conducting an end of project review (or end of stage)

ABCDE gives a framework for reviewing a project with your team so you learn lessons for future projects. This can be done at the end of a key stage on a longer project so that you learn lessons for the next stage of the project. It is an opportunity for you to show your appreciation for the team members' efforts, to acknowledge their contribution and to congratulate them on successes. It need not take long – 15 minutes spent on this is better than no time! Half an hour is even more productive and can save many times that on future projects.

<table>
<tr><td>A</td><td>Achieve: What did we achieve?<br>Review what the stage/project has achieved in comparison to the planned outcomes. This could include:<br>• Objectives<br>• Key deliverables<br>• Meeting of deadlines<br>• Financial targets<br>• Quality standards<br>• Reduction of risks<br>• Client satisfaction levels<br>• Market reputation<br>• New expertise and contacts for the team.</td></tr>
<tr><td>B</td><td>Benefits: Which benefits have been delivered?<br>Review whether the anticipated benefits for the client and other stakeholders were delivered and what evidence there is to support this view.<br>It may be too soon for some benefits to be reviewed or be visible. If this is the case plan how and when you will review and report on these benefits. This can create opportunities to keep in touch with clients between projects.</td></tr>
<tr><td>C</td><td>Clarify: What went well on the project, what steps were successful?<br>In this section ask the team to brainstorm a list of what went well on the project. Use a flipchart to collect ideas and keep the pace fast. Ask if you did the project again, what would you like to see done in the same way because it worked so well? After initial ideas, you can prompt the team by asking them what worked well in relation to any of the following not already covered:</td></tr>
</table>

<table>
<tr><td></td><td>

- Communication
- Co-ordination across the team
- Decision making and escalation of issues
- Dealing with the client, other parties and other stakeholders
- Managing the timetable
- Getting support and resources
- Use of technology
- Use of the team's project management systems, tracking documents or processes
- Managing the budget.

</td></tr>
<tr><td>D</td><td>

***Difficulties:*** **What difficulties did we have to overcome?**

Cover the negatives in the middle of the meeting so you start and finish positively. Brainstorm a list of all the things which didn't go as well as expected or which created difficulties on the project. Then discuss:

- Could these things have been anticipated?
- Were they handled effectively?
- What lessons can be learned for the next stage/future projects so these difficulties can be avoided?

Prompt the team with questions such as:

- What could we have been done better, faster or more cheaply?
- What work was wasted or not appreciated by the client or other stakeholders?
- What else could be done to improve our efficiency?
- What else would help us to work together more effectively?
- What else would improve the quality of service we delivered?
- What would have made our work easier?
- What would make it more rewarding or satisfying to work on a similar project in the future?

</td></tr>
<tr><td>E</td><td>

***Evaluate:*** **What lessons are there for the next stage/future projects?**

- Review the lists you have generated and identify and prioritize any lessons learned for the next stage/future projects.
- Identify any ideas which need further development and how these will be taken forwards.
- Agree how you will document these lessons learned so they can be used on future projects.
- Agree what would be beneficial to share with other teams in the firm.
- Plan how on the next project you will evaluate whether this has resulted in improvements in the way you deliver projects.

</td></tr>
</table>

# Part 5

# Tools for one-to-one performance conversations

# Introduction

Often lawyers think that performance conversations are only needed to manage problems. That's not true. They are about setting clear expectations and giving timely and helpful feedback so that team members can deliver the level of performance needed and fulfil their potential. They are positive conversations that motivate and build trust. Too often, however, these conversations are neglected. Task-focused leaders don't prioritize them and even people-focused leaders struggle to find adequate time for them. This toolkit will make you more efficient and ensure that your conversations are both clear and encouraging.

Such conversations are the bedrock for building a great team. However, they also need to be supplemented with a planned approach to managing people. In addition, you need to:

- **Recruit the right people**: You may have inherited your team, but you will also have opportunities to recruit when the team grows or if people leave. Use this as an opportunity to build a team that not only has the expertise you need, but also the diversity required for a healthy balance. When interviewing, it is essential that you look for evidence of how that person is likely to behave in the role as well as of their expertise and intelligence. Using the 'Tell me about a time when you had to … [deal with an angry client/cope with excessive workload/deliver against an aggressive deadline/give difficult feedback etc.] …' will glean more useful insights than asking questions such as 'How would you [deal with an angry client, etc.]?' where it is too easy to give a text book answer. The quality of your questions and interest in them will sell the firm better than any fireside chat and will help you make more informed decisions.
- **Retain talent**: Lawyers no longer stay with one firm or in one job from the start of their career until they retire. Therefore, it is critical they have job satisfaction, a career trajectory that matches their expectations and the sense that they are fairly rewarded for their efforts and achievements. On top of this, most lawyers want to know that the leaders they work for care

about them and their career and not just about getting work done and keeping clients happy. This is why the quality of conversations you have with team members is so critical. It is a key weapon in your armoury for retaining talent. Many lawyers will stay in a firm that has lower tangible rewards, just because they are loyal to a leader that cares about them.

- **Allocate work fairly**: In many law firms this has become a focus of attention in the last decade. Work allocation is not just making sure work is done at the right level and profitably, but also about giving lawyers equal opportunities for development and profile. In some firms, work allocation managers now distribute work so that partners can no longer dish out assignments to their favourites. When allocating work, always think about resolving the tension between getting a job done quickly by someone who is experienced versus investing time in developing a team member and giving them opportunities to develop expertise and contacts. Balance the short term with the longer term.
- **Plan development**: There are lots of sophisticated tools that can help you plan the development of team members from agreed descriptions of what you should expect at each level (expectations or competency frameworks), to objective setting and tracking systems, to ways of identifying high potentials for development such as the 9-box talent matrix. However, if you take everything back to basics, it is about having an open dialogue and honest conversation with your team members about what is expected at the next stage and their aspirations. To encourage more of these conversations to take place, many firms have introduced mentoring and sponsorship schemes to separate development conversations from performance conversations with their 'line-manager'. The feedback and coaching tools in this toolkit can be used when you are mentoring someone as well as when managing your own team members.
- **Review performance**: Performance should be reviewed regularly but until a few years ago most law firms would rely on an annual appraisal – often disliked by both partners and team members. HR departments tried to make it easier and fairer by providing guidance for ratings, benchmarking

meetings for greater consistency across the firm, and some introduced forced distribution curves to avoid the problem of over generous rating. Now, however, many firms have decided that all the effort isn't doing as much to enhance performance compared to more regular and less formal conversations. The current trend is for three-monthly check-ins with short-term objectives that can be delivered rather than annual objectives which sit in a drawer for the next 11 months.

This is the tip of the iceberg for each of these topics! Your HR department should have policies and expertise to help you do these things effectively. However, after years of working with lawyers, I firmly believe that it is the quality of the conversation that counts. HR systems are helpful, and essential for fairness in larger firms, but are of little value unless leaders have engaging conversations about performance with their team members.

This toolkit provides a series of **ABCDE** tools to help you have those engaging conversations with your team members in a variety of situations. Each tool gets you to think about:

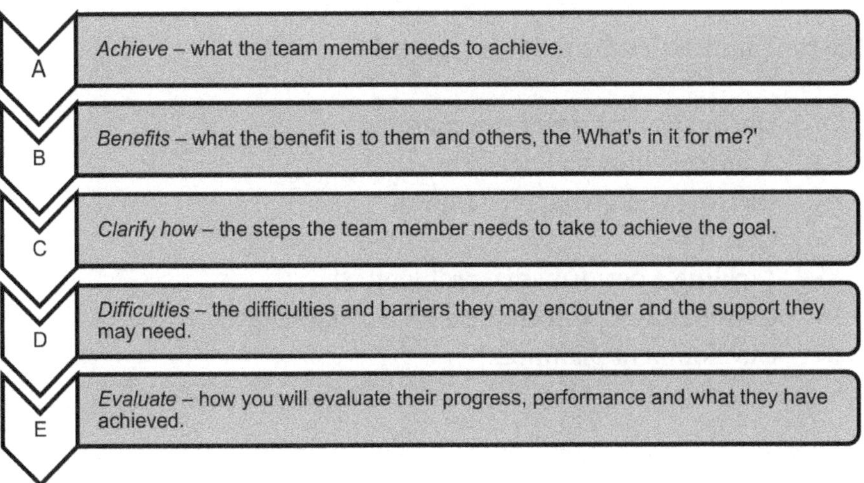


As with the project conversation tools, pay attention to the sections that you might usually ignore or not prioritize because of your preferred leadership style. Also consider and focus on those sections that may be particularly motivating for the team member and others which they may gloss over.

| **If your team member is** | **They will be listening for** | **Help them do well by** |
|---|---|---|
| Results-Driven | *Achieve* – the goal or target | Agreeing how they are going to achieve the goal: the **C, D** and **E** and, if the goal is not exciting to them, the **B** of why it's important to others. |
| Relationship-Focused | *Benefits* – why it's important | Focusing them on the end goal – **A**chieve – and ensuring they have thought through how much time it will take and other possible **D**ifficulties. |
| Security-Oriented | *Clarify how* – the steps for implementation | Create focus and urgency by highlighting **A**chieve, **B**enefits and how you will regularly **Evaluate** progress. When discussing **C**, highlight what is different to normal and any corners which can be cut. |
| Risk-Averse | *Difficulties* – to overcome | **A**chieve and **B**enefits to provide the bigger picture and when discussing **C** highlight what can be excluded, the level of detail required, the level of risk that is acceptable. |

The toolkit includes the following tools for:

- On-boarding a new team member
- Adjusting how you delegate
- Praising and giving recognition
- Coaching
- Tackling a performance problem
- Conducting a performance review meeting
- Development planning

# On-boarding a new team member

You can use the **ABCDE** approach when welcoming a new joiner to your team and ensuring that they are clear what is expected of them in their role. The clearer you make your expectations, the easier it will be for the new joiner to create a good first impression. Also, it will be easier for you to give feedback if the new joiner is not meeting your expectations for performance.

What is covered will depend on the seniority of the new joiner and what was discussed during the recruitment process. However, it is worth repeating some things, to make the link between what was offered and the reality of the job. This prevents a new joiner becoming anxious or cynical.

Make it a dialogue so that the team member learns about you and the team and you learn about them.

| | |
|---|---|
| A | ***Achieve:* This is what we aim to achieve in this team...**<br>Provide the context for the new joiner's role by describing:<br>• The overall aims of the team and how this contributes to what the firm is trying to achieve; how the aims link with the firm's strategy, values, brand and culture<br>• Key clients and what the team is trying to achieve with these<br>• How the new joiner's role fits in and how you want them to contribute to the team's aims<br>• Key success factors for the role.<br>Ask what the new joiner most wants to achieve in the role, where they think they can make their best contribution.<br>Agree focus, priorities and a couple of objectives for the first three–six months. |
| B | ***Benefits:* These will be the benefits...**<br>It is important to enthuse the new joiner and reinforce that they have made the right decision in joining the team. Describe:<br>• How the firm values what your team delivers<br>• The opportunities for interesting and high quality work<br>• Development opportunities<br>• How the role will progress if appropriate |

| | |
|---|---|
| | Briefly describe what you enjoy about the work/team and how this links with your values.<br><br>Ask the new joiner what they are hoping to gain from working in this role and team; what gives them job satisfaction. |
| C | ***Clarify:* Let me clarify what we expect of people working in the team**<br><br>If the new joiner is to get off to a good start, they need to understand the written and unwritten rules of working effectively in the team. Some of this may be covered in your firm's induction procedures; if so focus on how things work in your team. The clearer someone is on these working practices, the easier it is for them to get off to a good start and for you to give quick feedback if they behave in a way that contravenes team norms.<br><br>• Service: speed of response, availability and telephone handling<br>• Calendar/diary management, email management, filing<br>• Supervision, quality controls, review procedures<br>• Use of team resources, templates, technology<br>• Internet use and protocols<br>• How to work with colleagues and different personalities in the team, respecting differences, collaborating<br>• Keeping up-to-date, self-development, attending training and team meetings<br>• Budget control, time-recording, timekeeping, absences, holidays, expenses. |
| D | ***Difficulties:* Let's discuss any difficulties you anticipate in settling in and how we can support you in getting off to a good start**<br><br>It is important to establish an open dialogue with the new joiner so that they can be honest about areas where they may lack experience or confidence. Agree how the new joiner's concerns will be handled and what support to provide e.g. a 'buddy' in the team, on-the-job training for any unfamiliar areas of expertise. |
| E | ***Evaluate:* Let's plan how we will check you are settling in well**<br><br>Finish on an enthusiastic note, saying how pleased you are they have joined the team, the importance of their contribution and how you will check they are getting off to a good start:<br><br>• Agree when you will meet to discuss how they are settling in (within one–two weeks)<br>• Agree a first review (e.g. after two–three months) when you will give feedback on how they are doing so far and so you can review progress with initial objectives<br>• Explain any procedures for assessing performance before the end of the probation period<br>• Explain how these reviews will fit with the firm's ongoing performance review process and goal setting. For example, whether you have quarterly check-ins, annual reviews, etc. |

# Adjusting how you delegate

When delegating, flex your supervision approach for each stage of the **ABCDE** to give the right amount of instruction and support needed depending on the team member's level of experience for the task, their confidence to act alone and their motivation to prioritise the task. Choose from the five approaches below.

| **Inexperienced** | | **Experienced** | | |
|---|---|---|---|---|
| **Train/tell (sat nav)** | **Brainstorm and coach** | **Reassure** | **Motivate/sell** | **Delegate and let go** |
| Use for novices, when they don't know where or how to start. | Use for keen learners who have a little experience on which to build. | Use for cautious intermediates. You can trust them to know what to do, but they lack confidence to act independently. | Use for jaded experts or those juggling conflicting priorities. They know what to do but you can't trust them to get it done on time or to the standard required. | Use for self-reliant experts. You can trust them as they are experienced, confident and motivated to get it done. |
| Hands on | | | | Hands off |
| Maximum supervision | | | | Minimum supervision |
| Minimum autonomy | | | | Maximum autonomy |

Whatever supervision approach you use, by the end of each stage of the **ABCDE** your team member should:

***Achieve:*** have a clear goal, what needs to be achieved on the task/project and any personal development goal

***Benefits:*** be motivated by the importance of the task/the benefits to them

***Clarify how:*** have a plan for completing the task/project: deliverables, steps, timetable, level of quality expected by you/client, resources, budget

***Difficulties:*** be aware of risks to manage and what support they may need

***Evaluate:*** have agreed how much monitoring is needed and their responsibility for updating you

See the following table for a summary of the how to do the **ABCDE** for each supervision approach. For more guidance See Part 1 Clarify How.

You may also need to tweak your supervision approach to adjust to your team member's personality; a second table summarises how to do this.

A final table shows how your own style preferences can trap you into using the wrong approach for the situation.

## ABCDE for each supervision approach

| Inexperienced | | Experienced | | |
|---|---|---|---|---|
| **Train/tell (sat nav)** | **Brainstorm and coach** | **Reassure** | **Motivate/sell** | **Delegate and let go** |
| Use for novices, when they don't know where or how to start. | Use for keen learners who have a little experience on which to build. | Use for cautious intermediates. You can trust them to know what to do, but they lack confidence to act independently. | Use for jaded experts or those juggling conflicting priorities. They know what to do but you can't trust them to get it done on time or to the standard required. | Use for self-reliant experts. You can trust them as they are experienced, confident and motivated to get it done. |
| **A:** Set a clear goal for achieving the task and for learning. | **A:** Set a clear goal for achieving the task and for learning. | **A:** Ask them to suggest a goal for taking ownership. | **A:** Ask them to suggest a goal for delivering to quality/ timeframe required. | **A:** Ask them to set their own challenging goal eg for profitability, profile or self-development. |
| **B:** Explain what they will learn and why the task is important. | **B:** Explain what they will learn, the progress they will make and why the task is important. | **B:** Discuss how it will help them grow more confident to act alone. | **B:** Discuss why the task is so important, why you need to rely on them and identify benefits for them (as well as others). | **B:** Discuss any relevant benefit they might gain e.g. ownership, responsibility, profile, adding to track record or network. |
| **C:** Provide the action plan with clear steps and detailed instructions. | **C:** Brainstorm and ask questions to help them produce a clear plan. | **C:** Ask them to create a plan for you to review – confirm/adjust as needed. | **C:** Ask them to create a timetable and overview plan for you to review. Negotiate changes if necessary. | **C:** Allow them to determine their approach, create their own plan. |
| **D:** Explain how to avoid difficulties and when you want them to come to you to check or for support. | **D:** Ask them to anticipate difficulties and risks – add to these where there are gaps. Discuss how to address the difficulties and when your support will be required. | **D:** Ask them to think what issues they might need to escalate to you and check what support they might need to overcome difficulties they anticipate. | **D:** Check what could stop them delivering on time and to the standard needed. Negotiate if necessary. | **D:** Say you will be available if needed. |
| **E:** Explain how you will check progress at each step of the plan. Ask them to come back if they are unsure how to proceed. | **E:** Agree how frequently you will monitor progress, encourage them to alert you early if anything is likely to hold up the project. | **E:** Agree light touch monitoring: ask them to report to you on progress at key points. | **E:** Agree the frequency and how they will report on progress. Increase frequency if your trust levels drop. | **E:** Agree to monitor at end or at key points on long projects. |

## Tweak your approach for their style preferences

Select the relevant approach but be aware that different personalities like being supervised in different ways so a little tweaking may be necessary

| **Inexperienced** | | **Experienced** | | |
|---|---|---|---|---|
| **Train/tell (sat nav)** | **Brainstorm and coach** | **Reassure** | **Motivate/sell** | **Delegate and let go** |
| For novices | For learners with a little experience | For cautious intermediates | For jaded experts or those with conflicting priorities | For self-reliant experts |
| Because the dialogue is rather one way, Results-Driven and Relationship-Focused team members can get a bit frustrated by the pace so move to brainstorming and coaching as quickly as you can.<br>For Risk-Averse and Security-Oriented team members the opposite is often true. They love the clarity and security of knowing how to do the perfect job and of following instructions to get there as easily as possible. Wean them off as soon as you can by moving to brainstorming and coaching. | Relationship-Focused and Results-Driven team members relish this style because they enjoy the pace and using their initiative. Once they have sufficient expertise, reduce the amount of time spent on upfront dialogue and get them planning on their own.<br>For Risk-Averse and Security-Oriented team members, give them time to think before expecting them to talk. They may be more reluctant to play with ideas. If you can, give them the context to read before the discussion so they can prepare. | Security-Oriented and Risk-Averse team members may like you to use this style for longer than is needed. Make them readier to act alone by explicitly saying they are ready and that you trust them.<br>For Results-Driven and Relationship-Focused team members you may find their outward confidence tricks you into using this style too soon. Let them get on with it, but make it easy for them to have access to you if they hit a problem. Make sure they don't neglect to report back to you. | Results-Driven and Risk-Averse team members may be more cynical about this approach. Highlight the importance of the task and of getting it done right rather than appealing to them to be helpful. Provide evidence of any benefits you suggest.<br>For Relationship-Focused and Security-Oriented team members highlight the value to the client and team - play on their desire to cooperate and collaborate and show who will appreciate their efforts. | Results-Driven team members love this style but may want you to use it too soon. If you need to provide more guidance and keep more control, explain your approach is to ensure they get the best results and speed up their development.<br>Relationship-Focused team members also love this style but they still need praise and recognition so don't ignore them just because they don't need your input.<br>Risk-Averse and Security-Oriented team members feel they are making a valuable contribution when working in a self-reliant way. Watch they don't get in a rut – make sure you give them work that will stretch them too as they may not ask for this. |

## Don’t fall into the trap of using the wrong approach

Beware of your own style preferences too which could trap you into using an inappropriate approach. Before delegating plan which supervision approach matches the situation and the team member, not the one you favour.

| Train/tell (sat nav) | Brainstorm and coach | Reassure | Motivate/sell | Delegate and let go |
|---|---|---|---|---|
| Favoured by Risk Averse leaders. Used by Results-Driven leaders when forced to work with someone they don’t trust. | Favoured by Relationship-Focused leaders. | Favoured by Security-Oriented leaders. | Favoured by Relationship-Focused leaders. | Favoured by Results-Driven leaders. |
| Used inappropriately, you may come across as a micro-manager. | Used with someone experienced, you may come across as patronizing. Used with a novice, you may come across as too challenging. | Used inappropriately, you may come across as too protective or distrustful. | Used inappropriately and excessively, you may come across as manipulative. | Used inappropriately, you may come across as aloof and uncaring. |

# Praising and giving recognition

**A**BC can be used to praise a team member and reinforce good performance. Praise is also a soft reward and motivates the person to repeat that level of performance. To keep it positive and succinct, use only **ABC** – there is no need to discuss **D** and **E**.

To be effective praise needs to:

- Be prompt
- Be sincere
- Reward achievement or progress
- Be commensurate with the level of achievement/progress.

| | |
|---|---|
| A | ***Achieve:* Describe the achievement**<br>Focus on the outcome which the team member has achieved.<br>Where appropriate, link this level of achievement to prior levels to highlight progress and build self-esteem. |
| B | ***Benefits:* Identify who has benefitted**<br>In describing the benefits you will show how you and others value what has been achieved, what difference it has made, for example, to:<br>• The project<br>• The client and other stakeholders<br>• You<br>• The team<br>• The firm<br>• The team member's reputation or profile<br>• The team member's expertise.<br>When appropriate, you can describe how it has reinforced important values in the firm or team.<br>Describing the benefits, makes the praise feel genuine and more than just a pat on the back. |

| C | *Clarify:* **Be clear and specific about what impressed you**<br>Be specific about what you think the team member did well – describe the actions or behaviours that contributed to the success or to the progress made. Where appropriate you can include how difficulties were overcome successfully.<br>This will focus the team member's attention on their own task-relevant behaviours or actions.<br>It will also clarify what the team member should repeat in future.<br>If you want to build on this success, you can ask the team member how they plan to use this approach on future assignments. |
|---|---|

# Coaching

ABCDE can be used to coach a team member, using questions to help the team member think for themselves what they want to do. It can be used in a range of situations including deciding on a course of action, tackling problems, planning development or next career moves and when mentoring.

The tool provides sample questions to facilitate their thinking.

| | |
|---|---|
| A | ***Achieve:* Agree a goal**<br>• What would you like to achieve?<br>• How will you know when you have achieved it?<br>• What would you like to happen that isn't happening now?<br>• What would you like to stop happening?<br>• If you had a magic wand, how would you use it to change things?<br>• In summary, what goal would you like to set? |
| B | ***Benefits:* Check if the goal is worthwhile**<br>• What will happen if you achieve this?<br>• On a scale of 1–10 how important is this to you? To others?<br>• How much do you really want this? Is it optional or essential?<br>• How aligned is your goal to the aims/strategy of your team?<br>• What will happen if you don't do this?<br>• What won't you be able to do if you focus on this? |
| C | ***Clarify how:* Plan the steps to get from the current situation to the goal**<br>• Where are you now in relation to your goal?<br>• What is happening at the moment?<br>• When and how often does this happen?<br>• What could you do to change the situation?<br>• What have you tried so far?<br>• What alternatives are there to this?<br>• What have you *not* tried so far?<br>• How might others approach this?<br>• Would you like some suggestions?<br>• Who might be able to help?<br>• What are the advantages/disadvantages of each approach?<br>• What action do you plan to take? How could you put this into an action plan? |

| | |
|---|---|
| D | ***Difficulties:* Consider what could get in the way of reaching the goal**<br>• What might stop you achieving this?<br>• What obstacles might you encounter?<br>• How could you get around these difficulties?<br>• What support do you need?<br>• How might you get this support? |
| E | ***Evaluate:* Plan how to review progress with the action plan**<br>• How and when will you put this into action?<br>• How will you check progress?<br>• How will you evaluate your success? |

# Tackling a performance problem

Use the **ABCDE** approach to plan constructive feedback which is both direct and supportive. Plan what you will say and the questions you will ask so that you can understand their perspective on what is causing the problem and their ideas for the solution. By the end they should be clear on how to change and feel that you have helped them.

The tool can be used for quick, informal pieces of feedback, the first time you notice something going wrong. In these instances keep it light touch and future-focused – a tip for next time. If a problem persists, you will need to plan carefully for a longer and more thorough conversation so that they are clear what needs to change and the consequences of not doing so. In extreme cases this might be failing to progress to the next stage, not being chosen to work with that client again, etc.

When you have a good team member, you may be reluctant to tackle a problem since you don't want to upset them or damage your relationship. However, this isn't fair to them – they would rather know now so that they can improve quickly, than wait to find out at a review. Keep the tone positive and supportive and they will thank you for helping them be the best that they can be.

<table>
<tr><td>A</td><td>Achieve: Discuss and agree what needs to be achieved<br>• Start in a non-threatening way such as 'I'd like to discuss how I can help you ....' Make this a positive statement or goal describing the level of performance you want to see. For example, 'I'd like to see you delegating more' or 'I'd like to see you giving me work which is ready to go to the client without me having to proof read it'.<br>• Use 'I' statements e.g. 'I'd like to see you doing ...' 'I expect you to ....'<br>• If the team member seems unaware of the problem, then describe what has gone wrong or how the team member is not achieving the level of performance expected.</td></tr>
</table>

| | |
|---|---|
| | • Describe the evidence that actions, behaviours or results are falling short of what you expect – be specific and objective. To do this use the phrase 'I noticed you …' so that your feedback is descriptive and informative, not judgemental. For example, 'I was expecting you to involve the junior associate, but notice you have done all the work on this yourself' or 'I noticed there were three typos on the first page'.<br>• Ask questions to understand the team member's perspective of the problem. Use open questions such as 'How do you …?' 'Tell me how you approach this.' 'What stops you doing this?' 'What concerns have you had about this?' For example 'What stopped you delegating to the junior associate?' or 'How do you check your work before handing it to me to review?'<br>• Empathise where appropriate, for example sharing when you have experienced the same difficulty or when others have.<br>• Agree on what the problem is and what is causing it.<br>• Agree a goal for improvement – what to achieve. |
| B | ***Benefits:* Agree the benefits of changing/improving to motivate the team member**<br>• Discuss the benefits of changing or of making an improvement: for the team member and their reputation/future opportunities, for you, for the client, for others, for the team, for the firm – as appropriate.<br>• If they don't appear keen to change, it may be necessary to describe the negative impact the problem is having on others at the moment. You could ask them to think how their actions might be perceived by others, how it affects their reputation.<br>• If a problem is severe, discuss what is at stake and any consequences.<br>• By the end of this stage the team member should agree it is worthwhile improving their performance in the area discussed. |
| C | ***Clarify:* Agree clear action to solve the problem/improve performance**<br>• Avoid being prescriptive, telling them how to change. Ask for their ideas on how to improve/change/move forwards.<br>• Encourage them to come up with their own solutions first by asking one or two questions such as:<br>▪ What will you do differently next time?<br>▪ With the benefit of hindsight, what would you change?<br>▪ How can we avoid this happening again?<br>▪ What would help you to …?<br>▪ How could you …?<br>▪ What could I do that would help you?<br>• Help them develop their ideas into practical solutions.<br>• If they are stuck: describe what it would look like if the team member were doing what you expected; provide tips and advice and check whether this would work for them.<br>• Agree together what the team member is going to do – be specific. |

| | |
|---|---|
| D | *Difficulties:* **Plan how to avoid any difficulties and any support required**<br>• Make sure that nothing will undermine the team member's efforts to improve by asking questions such as:<br>▪ What could get in the way of making progress on this?<br>▪ What could stop you achieving this?<br>▪ How could we avoid these/work around these?<br>• Agree any support needed. |
| E | *Evaluate:* **Agree how and when you will evaluate progress**<br>• Summarize what you are expecting by making the action/outcome specific and measurable or by setting a SMART objective (Specific, Measurable, Agreed, Realistic, Time-bound).<br>• Where appropriate ask the team member to create an action plan listing the steps they (and you) are going to take and by when so that you can monitor progress.<br>• Agree when and how you will review progress with the action plan/agreed changes. |

# Conducting a performance review meeting

ABCDE can be used to conduct a performance review or quarterly check-in. **A** and **B** are used to review performance over the last year/period. **C, D** and **E** are used to plan for the year/period ahead and at least 70% of the time should be spent on this.

Use questions to get the team member talking and participating in the review – this increases the perception of fairness and usefulness of the review.

| | |
|---|---|
| A | ***Achieve:* Focus on what has been achieved in the last period**<br>Discuss performance in the past year or period – this should be a summary of feedback already provided.<br>• What achievements are you most proud of this year/quarter?<br>• This is what we think you have achieved ...<br>• This is what most impressed us ...<br>• This is the progress we noticed ...<br>• Where didn't you achieve as much as you were hoping?<br>• This is where you didn't achieve what we were expecting ... What got in the way? |
| B | ***Benefits:* Focus on the value of the experience and contribution**<br>Provide praise and appreciation for what has been achieved and the contribution made.<br>• How have you benefitted from your experience this year/quarter?<br>• What have you learned?<br>• How has this added to your track record/reputation?<br>• How have clients/others benefitted?<br>• This is how we have benefitted from your contribution ... Thank you! |

| | |
|---|---|
| C | ***Clarify:* Clarify expectations for the year/quarter ahead**<br>Plan for the year/quarter ahead and set new expectations.<br>• Clarify how to build on strengths/skills/experience.<br>• Clarify any changes needed to meet expectations for performance.<br>• Clarify how to step up to the next level if nearing promotion.<br>• Clarify challenges ahead and plan how to meet them.<br>• Clarify changes to the role or working practices.<br>• Clarify aspirations: What do you want to achieve in the year ahead/in your career? |
| D | ***Difficulties:* Ask about any difficulties or concerns**<br>Provide an opportunity for the team member to air any difficulties or concerns.<br>• What difficulties are you experiencing in the role?<br>• What suggestions do you have for improving the situation?<br>• What concerns do you have about the year/quarter ahead?<br>• What difficulties might you face in realizing your career aspirations?<br>• What action will help you to overcome these difficulties?<br>• What do you need from me?<br>• What one thing could I do differently to help us work together even better? |
| E | ***Evaluate:* Agree key objectives for the next period and how to evaluate progress**<br>• Summarize: Your core message for the review.<br>• Agree objectives for the year ahead/next quarter.<br>• Agree how you will evaluate progress and success.<br>• Check: How enthusiastic are you feeling about the objectives we have agreed?<br>• Check: How enthusiastic are you feeling about the period ahead/your role? |

# Development planning

The following are two development planning templates based on **ABCDE**. You can use them with a team member for development planning either when coaching or planning how to take performance to the next level.

## Version 1:

| **Goals: What I would like to *Achieve* and the *Benefits* to me, my team, the firm** | **Where I am now** | **How I am going to do this (*Clarify* steps and how to avoid *Difficulties*)** | **By when** | **How I will *Evaluate* progress and outcomes; indicators of success** |
|---|---|---|---|---|
| | | | | |
| | | | | |
| | | | | |
| | | | | |
| | | | | |

## Version 2:

| | |
|---|---|
| ***Achieve:*** the end goal | |
| ***Benefits:*** the business case and personal benefits to my career | |
| ***Evaluate:*** indicators of success | |

| ***Clarify*** steps to take (and how to overcome ***Difficulties***) | | | | ***Evaluate*** |
|---|---|---|---|---|
| | What | When | Support/resources needed | Progress/status |
| 1 | | | | |
| 2 | | | | |
| 3 | | | | |
| 4 | | | | |

# Part 6
# Conclusion

# Conclusion and next steps

By now you should have started to notice the difference that adjusting your leadership style is making. What has been the impact on your projects? What have your team members noticed? Have you started to find 'difficult' people less challenging and are you even starting to appreciate their value better? In what ways are you now a better leader?

Adjusting your leadership style can feel strange at first, but you will find it increasingly easy and that's how great leaders become great – by experimenting with their approach, reviewing the results and then practising until it becomes second nature. This is how they get to be the best version of themselves they can be.

It is also where one-to-one coaching is, of course, a great help. A coach will keep you focused on adopting new practices and habits. Intellectually you know what you should do (you are bright!) but in the busy life of a lawyer it is easy to slip back into old ways of doing things.

When I'm coaching lawyers this dynamic plays out. We have a feedback session where they become very aware of their strengths and the changes that will make them more effective leaders. Then there is often an uncomfortable stage when the lawyer is very conscious of what they should be doing, they know when it's working but are also highly aware of when they are not doing it. Then gradually, as small changes bring success, the motivation to adopt new practices increases, they get bolder, they are struck by how much time they are saving and how much more effective they have become. They become more confident leaders.

If you don't have access to a coach, stay persistent, keep experimenting and learning. Trust the following process and be your own coach. Here's how to do it:

1. Identify three actions to take over the next month which you think will make you a more effective leader of teams. The actions should be things you will need to do anyway. For example, you might want to get better at motivating your team. If that's your goal identify three specific situations where you need to do this such as in an upcoming team meeting, or when delegating a task for a demanding client or giving feedback to someone

who has just completed a piece of work. For each situation plan what you are going to do – the action you will take, including how to adjust to the individual's style.

2. After each one of these actions have been completed, stop and reflect for two minutes: What went well? What was challenging? What have I learned?
3. At the end of the month, sit down and do a 15-minute self-review using the **ABCDE** approach.

   **A**: What have I ***Achieved*** this month in enhancing my leadership style?

   **B**: What have been the ***Benefits*** for me, my team, the clients, the firm?

   **C**: What three actions will I take over the next month to help me do this more often, or to become a better leader in another way?

   **D**: What will stop me achieving these and what do I need to do or what support do I need to enable me to succeed (this might include scaling back your plan if it is too ambitious)?

   **E**: How will I know if I have succeeded? What will I be measuring myself against when I look back at the end of the month to evaluate my progress?

4. Then repeat the process for about six months.

Use the same approach if you go on a leadership development programme. Too often it is easy to leave enthused, then shut the manual and go back to business as usual. Instead, coach yourself so that you implement the behaviours that you have identified will make you more effective. Your takeaways are bound to be different from other participants on the same programme, but it can help to buddy up with someone and compare notes of what you have achieved over the next three–six months. Practise a little peer coaching with each other – use the **ABCDE** coaching tool.

The aim of this book was to help you benefit from my experience of coaching and developing lawyers over the past 25 years, especially if you don't have access to coaching or a leadership development programme. I hope you have found it inspiring. If you would like more tailored tips for your own style and situation, or if you would like more support then please contact me at sallysanderson@profexconsulting.com.

# About Sally Sanderson

This book is based on Sally's experience in developing and coaching lawyers.

Sally is a multi-award-winning consultant to law firms. She has over 25 years of experience of developing lawyers through workshops and coaching, using psychometric assessments to increase self-awareness and speed up their development.

She specializes in leadership, emerging leaders, people and project management development programmes for lawyers (in private practice and in-house) and for business services directors and managers in law firms.

Her career has been spent developing professionals – initially at a global accountancy firm and then at a City law firm before setting up Profex Consulting in 2001. She works internationally and her clients include some of the world's largest law firms as well as niche practices.

She is a Fellow of the Chartered Institute of Personnel and Development and a speaker at national learning and development conferences.

# Appendix 1

# Completing a behavioural profile

There are a whole range of behavioural profiling tools on the market. It is very common for law firms to use the DISC, Insights Discovery® or Social Styles models – all based on four quadrants. They are used globally in business settings and for busy lawyers, they are quick to complete, quick to understand and easy to apply in practice. Most test providers will charge for an assessment and a feedback report. However, if you google the following tests, you can find companies that provide a free high level test (usually to entice you to buy a detailed one). You can also contact me if you would like to arrange an assessment at sallysanderson@profexconsulting.com.

## DISC (Dominance/Influence/Steadiness/Compliance)

DISC is a behavioural theory originally developed by William Moulton Marston. His two scales were: how active or passive someone is and how they react in hostile and favourable situations. His theory has been researched and developed further by several companies so that the findings are robust and meet the standards of the British Psychological Society. I use the Thomas International PPA (Personal Profile Analysis) version of DISC because it is easy to see combined strengths and preferences. You can find out more about the PPA at www.thomas.co/personal-profile-analysis-ppa

## Insights Discovery® (a registered trade mark of The Insights Group Limited)

Insights Discovery® is based on the work of Swiss psychologist Carl Jung and a broad range of psychometric models. The model uses a simple and accessible four colour model: Fiery Red, Sunshine Yellow, Earth Green and Cool Blue. Everyone has these four colour energies within them – including a lead colour energy or preference – and it is the combination of these energies which creates each unique personality. Insights Discovery® is certified by the British Psychological Society and approved by the European Federation of Psychologists Associations via the Occupational Test Tools Certification Mark. Find out more at www.insights.com/products/insights-discovery/

## Social Styles

Social Styles was originally developed by David Merrill and Roger Reid. It uses two scales: Assertiveness and Responsiveness resulting in four patterns of behaviour: Driving, Expressive, Amiable and Analytical. This is a widely used tool and free-to-use tests are available on the internet.

Here is a summary of the profiling tools and how they link with the leadership styles in this book:

| **Profiling tool** | **Results-Driven** | **Relationship-Focused** | **Security-Oriented** | **Risk-Averse** |
| --- | --- | --- | --- | --- |
| DISC (Personal Profile Analysis) | Dominance | Influence | Steadiness | Compliance |
| Insights Discovery® | Fiery Red | Sunshine Yellow | Earth Green | Cool Blue |
| Social Styles | Driver | Expressive | Amiable | Analyser |

# Appendix 2

# ABCDE planner

This is a collection of the planning exercises in Part 1 so that you can use them whenever you are planning a project or an initiative.

## Achieve statement planner

Describe what you want the team/team member to achieve in fewer than 20 words.

- What's the end goal?
- What tangible result does the team or team member need to achieve?
- What will be an indicator that the team or person has succeeded?

(At this stage don't include why this goal is important.)

## Review your *Achieve* statement – is it:

- ✓ Succinct?
- ✓ Clear about the end result or goal?
- ✓ Specific?
- ✓ Tangible?
- ✓ Challenging but realistic?
- ✓ Positively expressed?

✓ Does it include an indicator of success?
✓ Will it be possible to monitor progress towards it?

## *Benefits* planner

List the ***Benefits*** to different stakeholders – why it is so important. To make a powerful case:

- Identify how different stakeholders will each benefit from the work
- Paint a picture
- Link the importance to something the stakeholder/team member values
- Use the 'so what this means for you' bridging phrase
- Provide evidence that the benefits are real and can be delivered.

| To the client/internal client |
|---|
| To the firm |
| To the team |
| To team members |

## Review your *Benefits* statements – do they:

✓ Overall, create a compelling sense of purpose for the team?
✓ Align to what is important to each stakeholder?
✓ Avoid any conflict of interest between different stakeholders?
✓ Describe something tangible or paint a picture such as:
  - Achievement of goals
  - Return on investment
  - Saved time

- Increased revenue or saved costs
- Decreased risk or hassle
- Improved market share, reputation or profile?

✓ Would it pass the test of a sceptic – can you provide proof?

## *Clarify how* planner

Identify the supervision approach style you should use to ***clarify how*** the work should be done.

| **Inexperienced** | | **Experienced** | | |
|---|---|---|---|---|
| **Train/tell (sat nav)** | **Brainstorm and coach** | **Reassure** | **Motivate/sell** | **Delegate and let go** |
| Use for novices, when they don't know where or how to start. | Use for keen learners who have a little experience on which to build. | Use for cautious intermediates. You can trust them to know what to do, but they lack confidence to act independently. | Use for jaded experts or those juggling conflicting priorities. They know what to do but you can't trust them to get it done on time or to the standard required. | Use for self-reliant experts. You can trust them as they are experienced, confident and motivated to get it done. |
| Maximum supervision<br>Minimum autonomy | | ⟷ | | Minimum supervision<br>Maximum autonomy |

Once you have selected the right supervision approach, plan what you will say or ask to create the plan with them or what you will check if the team is creating the plan themselves.

| ***Clarify how:*** | **What you will say/ask/check:** |
|---|---|
| 1. Steps to take to complete the work | |
| 2. Timetable and milestones | |

| 3. Budget/resources | |
|---|---|
| 4. Roles and responsibilities | |
| 5. How decisions will be made | |
| 6. How team members will communicate with each other and other stakeholders | |
| 7. How to meet quality standards | |

## Review your *Clarify how* plan – does the approach mean:

- ✓ You and the team will have a common understanding of how they will deliver the project?
- ✓ It will make it easy for you to monitor the team's progress?
- ✓ The discussions to create or review the plan will give you greater confidence in the team's ability and drive to deliver the results?
- ✓ Your chosen approach will demonstrate appropriate levels of trust in or support for the team?
- ✓ Your chosen approach will motivate the team and give them confidence to proceed?

## *Difficulties* planner (risk management)

First, identify potential difficulties represented by risks:

| **Identify possible risks** | What is the **probability** that the risk will occur? Is it: *High/medium/low* | What is the **impact** if the risk occurs? Is it: *High/medium/low* | Plan how to **manage** significant risks: *Accept/avoid/reduce/share* |
|---|---|---|---|
| 1. Timing (deadlines, bottlenecks, matter dragging on) | | | |
| 2. Staffing/resourcing | | | |
| 3. Financial (fees exceed estimate, out of scope work) | | | |
| 4. Dissatisfied clients/damaged relationships | | | |
| 5. Commercial (loss of market share/loss of experts to competitor) | | | |
| 6. Reputational/liability (poor advice, missed deadlines) | | | |

## *Difficulties* planner (overcoming resistance)

Next place stakeholders on the chart depending on their level of resistance or support and how actively they will help or hinder the team's work.

| | | |
|---|---|---|
| **Supportive of the project** | **Passive support: *'Let it happen'***<br><br>What action can you take with these stakeholders to make their support more visible i.e. move them into 'Make it Happen'? | **Active support: *'Make it happen'***<br><br>How can you focus their support to win others over or help you deliver the project? |
| **Against the project** | **Passive resistance: *'Ignore it happening'***<br><br>What action can you take with these stakeholders to win them over enough to at least move them to 'Let it Happen'? | **Active resistance: *'Stop it happening'***<br><br>Plan how to neutralize their objections – it may be sufficient to just move them to 'Ignore it'. |
| | **Passive:** less likely to demonstrate their support or resistance | **Active:** likely to act on their support or resistance |

## Review your *Difficulties* plan (for risk and resistance:

- ✓ Have you thought of both short-term and longer-term difficulties?
- ✓ If you ran the project plans past someone who is less enthusiastic, would they identify additional risks or resistance?
- ✓ Are your plans for overcoming any risks specific?

✓ Will it be easy for you to monitor and report on how risks are being managed?
✓ Will your plans for communicating with stakeholders address any resistance or make support more visible?
✓ What quick wins will you be able to achieve to win more support?

## *Evaluate* planner

Start by identifying how you will evaluate and report on progress – for regular reporting:

| **Regular reporting planner** | | | |
|---|---|---|---|
| **Who – key stakeholders for regular reporting:** | **When – frequency of reporting:**<br>• Daily<br>• Weekly<br>• Fortnightly<br>• Monthly<br>• At end of stage | **How – most appropriate format of status report**<br>• Email<br>• Call<br>• Meeting<br>• Tracker | **Focus of report – progress on:**<br>• Activities<br>• Issues/risks<br>• Timetable<br>• Financials |
| **Core team** | | | |
| **Extended team** | | | |
| **Client** | | | |
| **Internal management** | | | |

Next consider how you will review success at the end of stage and end of project to learn lessons for the next stage or the next project.

| | **Lessons learned planner** | | |
|---|---|---|---|
| | **Who to involve:** *Team/client/other stakeholders* | **Format:** *Call/meeting/ survey/facilitated meeting or workshop* | **Items to discuss to learn lessons for the next stage of the project or for other projects:** *Objectives met/benefits/financials/ team efficiency/communication/client satisfaction/know how and learning* |
| **End of stage** | | | |
| **End of project** | | | |

## Review your *Evaluate* plans – will they:

- ✓ Help you motivate the team and ensure they focus effort on the right things?
- ✓ Be feasible when you are busy/working on multiple projects?
- ✓ Make it easy to delegate some of the monitoring?
- ✓ Enhance client satisfaction?
- ✓ Ensure lessons learned will help the team deliver even better results next time?

# Appendix 3

# Additional resources

## Lessons for leaders from neuroscience

You will see from the footnotes that I am a big fan of understanding how the brain works – lessons from neuroscience. To find out more, in an easily digestible format I recommend:

*Your Brain at Work* by Dr David Rock, Harper Business (2009).
This is an entertaining read following a dual career couple at work. Rock points out that if they had a better understanding of how their brain works then they would know how to be more focused, organized, energized and effective. It includes his SCARF model which is an essential for all leaders. Not enough time to read a book, then for a quick introduction to SCARF watch the 3.5-minute video animation on YouTube: www.youtube.com/watch?v=qMejNf0dL2g

*Drive: The Surprising Truth About What Motivates Us* by Daniel H. Pink, Penguin Books Ltd (2009).
A book to challenge the way you think about motivating others. No more carrots and sticks, you need to focus on Autonomy, Mastery and Purpose – all very relevant for lawyers who do complex tasks.

## Leading international teams

Many lawyers find themselves leading teams of people from different jurisdictions and working with clients from other cultures. This requires a whole additional level of adjustment to be effective. *When Cultures Collide – Leading Across Cultures* by R. D. Lewis, Nicholas Brealey International (2006) is practical with chapters providing an introductory guide for different countries.

## Being an assertive leader

Many lawyers struggle with being direct and assertive but many books on assertiveness are not geared to business life. Try the very practical *Assertiveness at Work* by Ken and Kate Back, McGraw Hill (2005).

If you haven't come across Amy Cuddy's presentation on using body language to boost your confidence and authority on TED, watch it: it's a quick fix. https://www.ted.com/talks/amy_cuddy_your_body_language_may_shape_who_you_are

# Acknowledgements

If it had not been for my clients, this book would never have been written. I particularly want to thank Yvonne Garricks for first urging me to write a book on the **ABCDE** model and Joanne Gubbay for her support while I developed the model further. Her encouragement and feedback as my first reviewer proved invaluable.

The book would also never have been as rich in case study material if it had not been for all the lawyers I have profiled and coached over the years. I enjoyed working with you and hope that your experience, combined, anonymized and channeled through this book, will help other lawyers who may not have access to coaching and leadership development programmes.

Thank you also to all my other reviewers who gave generously of their time, especially when we all know what a premium value time has in law firms. Practising lawyers shared what they found most helpful and what would make it an easier book to dip into, especially William James and Simon Knott. Consultants on leadership and those managing law firms, especially Roger Wyn Jones, Neil May and Tony King, thank you for your detailed reviews and the reassurance that the book and toolkit are relevant and helpful for a wide range of professionals.

Finally, thank you to the Thomas International team for helping me to extract maximum value from their DISC Personal Profile Analysis over the years and to their Head of Science, Jason Darby, for confirming the way I have weaved together different psychometrics is valid.

# Index

## Case studies

*Leadership case studies*



*Team member case studies*



The case studies in the book are based on my experience of working with leaders in law firms and in-house legal teams. Each, however, is an amalgamation of more than one situation, more than one person and facts have been adapted – so they are fictitious and no resemblance to real life partners or leaders is intended. They are often presented without gender (and I use 'they' as the pronoun instead of 'he/ she') and from diverse backgrounds. The aim is to illustrate what happens in practice across the legal globe and to help readers identify with common challenges lawyers face.